Solidity Programming Essentials

A beginner's guide to build smart contracts for Ethereum and blockchain

Ritesh Modi

BIRMINGHAM - MUMBAI

Solidity Programming Essentials

Commissioning Editor: Merint Methew
Acquisition Editor: Sandeep Mishra
Content Development Editor: Priyanka Sawant
Technical Editor: Vibhuti Gawde
Copy Editor: Safis Editing
Project Coordinator: Vaidehi Sawant
Proofreader: Safis Editing
Indexer: Rekha Nair
Graphics: Jason Monteiro
Production Coordinator: Deepika Naik

First published: April 2018

Production reference: 1180418

Published by Packt Publishing Ltd.
Livery Place
35 Livery Street
Birmingham
B3 2PB, UK.

ISBN 978-1-78883-138-3

www.packtpub.com

`mapt.io`

Mapt is an online digital library that gives you full access to over 5,000 books and videos, as well as industry leading tools to help you plan your personal development and advance your career. For more information, please visit our website.

Why subscribe?

- Spend less time learning and more time coding with practical eBooks and Videos from over 4,000 industry professionals

- Improve your learning with Skill Plans built especially for you

- Get a free eBook or video every month

- Mapt is fully searchable

- Copy and paste, print, and bookmark content

PacktPub.com

Did you know that Packt offers eBook versions of every book published, with PDF and ePub files available? You can upgrade to the eBook version at `www.PacktPub.com` and as a print book customer, you are entitled to a discount on the eBook copy. Get in touch with us at `service@packtpub.com` for more details.

At `www.PacktPub.com`, you can also read a collection of free technical articles, sign up for a range of free newsletters, and receive exclusive discounts and offers on Packt books and eBooks.

Contributors

About the author

Ritesh Modi is an ex Microsoft senior technology evangelist and Microsoft regional lead. He has worked on Ethereum and Solidity, extensively helping and advising companies. Ritesh is a regular speaker on blockchain and Solidity at conferences and local meetups. He is an architect, evangelist, speaker, and a known leader for his contributions toward blockchain, data centers, Azure Bots, cognitive services, DevOps, Artificial Intelligence, and automation. He is the author of five books.

I have personally grown into a person who has more patience, perseverance, and tenacity while writing this book. I must thank the people who mean the world to me. I am talking about my mother, Bimla Modi, my wife, Sangeeta Modi, and my daughter, Avni Modi. I also thank the Packt team for their support.

About the reviewer

Pablo Ruiz has been involved in the creation of dozens of tech products over the past 12 years, working with the latest, cutting-edge technologies. In 2008, he became deeply involved in the creation of mobile games and applications; later on, he participated in many projects as an advisor or investor in the digital space. During 2015/2016, he was a director at one of the top venture capital firms in Latin America, where he built their Fintech ecosystem from the ground up. In 2018, after actively working on several ICOs, he joined Polymath as their VP of engineering to lead the development of the first Ethereum-based platform for issuing regulatory-compliant security tokens.

Packt is searching for authors like you

If you're interested in becoming an author for Packt, please visit `authors.packtpub.com` and apply today. We have worked with thousands of developers and tech professionals, just like you, to help them share their insight with the global tech community. You can make a general application, apply for a specific hot topic that we are recruiting an author for, or submit your own idea.

Table of Contents

Preface

I am not sure the last time I heard so much of a discussion about a technology across governments, organizations, communities, and individuals. Blockchain is a technology that is being discussed and debated at length across the world and organizations, and without a reason. Blockchain is not just a technology that has limited effect on our life. It has and will have widespread ramifications in our lives. The day is not far when blockchain will touch almost each aspect of our activities—whether paying bills, transactions with any organizations, getting salary, identity, educational results, activities, and so on. This is just the beginning, and we have just started to understand the meaning of decentralization and its impact.

I have been working on blockchain for quite some time now and have been a crypto-investor for long. I am a technologist and am completely fascinated by Bitcoin because of the architectural marvel it is. I have never come across such superior thought process and architecture that actually solves not only economic and social problems but solves some technically unsolved problems such as Byzantine general problems and fault tolerance. It solves the problem of distributed computing at large.

Ethereum is built in an almost similar fashion, and I was in awe when I first heard and experienced smart contracts. Smart contracts are one of the greatest innovation to deploy decentralized applications on blockchain and extend it easily with custom logic, policies, and rules.

I have thoroughly enjoyed authoring this book and sincerely hope that you would also enjoy reading and implementing Solidity. I have brought in a lot of my Solidity experience and try to make the maximum out of it. I hope this book makes you a better Solidity developer and a superior programmer.

Do let me know if there is anything I can do to make your experience better with this book. I am all ears, and happy learning!

Who this book is for

To make usage of the content of this book, basic prior knowledge of computing and general programming concepts is needed. If you feel you don't have that knowledge, it is always possible to catch up the basic requirements with a fast reading on many beginners' books on programming. This book is essentially intended for blockchain architects, developers, consultants, and IT engineers who are using blockchain to provide advanced services to end customers and employers. If you are also willing to write smart contracts solution on Ethereum, then this book is ideal for you. If you already have some experience with JavaScript, this book can help you speed up with it in a fast-paced way.

What this book covers

Chapter 1, *Introduction to Blockchain, Ethereum, and Smart Contracts*, takes you through the fundamentals of blockchain, its terminology and jargon, advantages, problems it's trying to solve, and industry relevance. It will explain the important concepts and architecture in detail. This chapter will also teach you about concepts specific to Ethereum. In this chapter, details about its concepts like externally owned accounts, contract accounts, its currency in terms of gas and Ether will be discussed. Ethereum is heavily based on cryptography and you'll also learn about hash, encryption, and usage of keys for creating transactions and accounts. How are transactions and accounts created, how gas is paid for each transaction, difference between message calls and transactions, and storage of code and state management will be explained in detailed.

Chapter 2, *Installing Ethereum and Solidity*, takes you through creating a private blockchain using Ethereum platform. It will provide step-by-step guidance for creating a private chain. Another important tool in Ethereum ecosystem is ganache-cli. This chapter will also show the process of installing ganache-cli and using it for deploying Solidity contracts, installing Solidity, and using it to compile Solidity contracts. You will also install Mist, which is a wallet and can interact with private chain. Mist will be used to create new accounts, deploy contracts, and use contracts. Mining of transactions will also be shown in this chapter. Remix is a great tool for authoring Solidity contracts.

Chapter 3, *Introducing Solidity*, begins the Solidity journey. In this chapter, you'll learn the basics of Solidity by understanding its different versions and how to use a version using pragmas. Another import aspect of this chapter is to understand the big picture of authoring smart contracts. Smart contract layout will be discussed in depth using important constructs like state variables, functions, constant function, events, modifiers, fallbacks, enums, and structs. This chapter discusses and implements the most important element of any programming language—data types and variables. There are data types that are simple and complex, value types and reference types, and storage and memory types—all these types of variables will also be shown using examples.

Chapter 4, *Global Variables and Functions*, provides implementation and usage details of block- and transaction-related global functions and variables and address- and contract-related global functions and variables. These comes in very handy in writing any series of smart contract development.

Chapter 5, *Expressions and Control Structures*, teaches you how to write contracts and functions that will have conditional logic using if...else and switch statements. Looping is an important part of any language and Solidity provides while and for loops for looping over arrays. Examples and implementation of looping will be part of this chapter. Loops must break based on certain conditions and should continue based on other conditions.

Chapter 6, *Writing Smart Contracts*, is the core chapter for the book. Here, you will start writing serious smart contracts. It will discuss the design aspects of writing smart contracts, defining and implementing a contract, and deploying and creating contracts using different mechanisms using the new keyword and using known addresses. Solidity provides rich object orientation, and this chapter will delve deep into object-oriented concepts and implementation such as inheritance, multiple inheritance, declaring abstract classes and interfaces, and providing method implementations to abstract functions and interfaces.

Chapter 7, *Functions, Modifiers, and Fallbacks*, shows how to implement basic functions that accept inputs and return outputs, functions that just output the existing state without changing the state and modifiers. Modifiers help in organizing code better in Solidity. It helps in security and reusing code within contracts. Fallbacks are important constructs and are executed when a function call does not match any of the existing function signatures. Fallbacks are also important for transferring Ether to contracts. Both modifiers and fallbacks will be discussed and implemented with examples for easy understanding.

Chapter 8, *Exceptions, Events, and Logging*, is important in Solidity from contract development perspective. Ether should be returned to caller in case of error and exception. Exception handling will be explained and implemented in depth in this chapter using newer Solidity constructs like assert, require, and revert. The hrow statement will also be discussed. Events and logging help in understanding the execution of contracts and functions. This chapter will show and explain the implementation for both events and logs.

Chapter 9, *Truffle Basics and Unit Testing*, covers the basics of truffle, understanding its concepts, creating a project and understanding its project structure, modifying its configuration, and taking a sample contract through entire life cycle of writing, testing, deploying, and migrating a contract. Testing is as important for contracts as writing a contract. Truffle helps in providing a framework to test; however, tests should be written. This chapter will discuss the basics of unit test, write unit test using Solidity, and execute those unit tests against the smart contract. Unit tests will be executed by creating transaction and validating its results. This chapter will show implementation details to write and execute unit tests for a sample contract.

Chapter 10, *Debugging Contracts*, will be show troubleshooting and debugging using multiple tools like Remix and events. This chapter will show how to execute code line by line, check state after every line of code, and change contract code accordingly.

To get the most out of this book

This book assumes a basic level knowledge of programming. It is ideal to have some background on any scripting language. All you need is an internet connectivity and a browser for using a majority of this book. There are sections that will need creating a machine to deploy blockchain specific tools and utilities. This machine can be physical or virtual, on cloud or on-premise.

Download the example code files

You can download the example code files for this book from your account at www.packtpub.com. If you purchased this book elsewhere, you can visit www.packtpub.com/support and register to have the files emailed directly to you.

You can download the code files by following these steps:

1. Log in or register at www.packtpub.com.
2. Select the **SUPPORT** tab.
3. Click on **Code Downloads & Errata**.
4. Enter the name of the book in the **Search** box and follow the onscreen instructions.

Once the file is downloaded, please make sure that you unzip or extract the folder using the latest version of:

- WinRAR/7-Zip for Windows
- Zipeg/iZip/UnRarX for Mac
- 7-Zip/PeaZip for Linux

The code bundle for the book is also hosted on GitHub at https://github.com/PacktPublishing/SolidityProgrammingEssentials. In case there's an update to the code, it will be updated on the existing GitHub repository.

We also have other code bundles from our rich catalog of books and videos available at https://github.com/PacktPublishing/. Check them out!

Conventions used

There are a number of text conventions used throughout this book.

CodeInText: Indicates code words in text, database table names, folder names, filenames, file extensions, pathnames, dummy URLs, user input, and Twitter handles. Here is an example: "A genesis.json file is required to create this first block."

A block of code is set as follows:

```
{
"config": {
"chainId": 15,
"homesteadBlock": 0,
"eip155Block": 0,
"eip158Block": 0
},
"nonce": "0x0000000000000042",
"mixhash":
"0x0000000000000000000000000000000000000000000000000000000000000000",
"difficulty": "0x200",
"alloc": {},
"coinbase": "0x0000000000000000000000000000000000000000",
"timestamp": "0x00",
"parentHash":
"0x0000000000000000000000000000000000000000000000000000000000000000",
"gasLimit": "0xffffffff",
"alloc": {
}
}
```

When we wish to draw your attention to a particular part of a code block, the relevant lines or items are set in bold:

```
[default]
exten => s,1,Dial(Zap/1|30)
exten => s,2,Voicemail(u100)
exten => s,102,Voicemail(b100)
exten => i,1,Voicemail(s0)
```

Any command-line input or output is written as follows:

```
npm install -g ganache-cli
```

Bold: Indicates a new term, an important word, or words that you see onscreen. For example, words in menus or dialog boxes appear in the text like this. Here is an example: "For sending Ether from one account to another, select an account and click on the **Send** button."

 Warnings or important notes appear like this.

Tips and tricks appear like this.

Get in touch

Feedback from our readers is always welcome.

General feedback: Email `feedback@packtpub.com` and mention the book title in the subject of your message. If you have questions about any aspect of this book, please email us at `questions@packtpub.com`.

Errata: Although we have taken every care to ensure the accuracy of our content, mistakes do happen. If you have found a mistake in this book, we would be grateful if you would report this to us. Please visit `www.packtpub.com/submit-errata`, selecting your book, clicking on the Errata Submission Form link, and entering the details.

Piracy: If you come across any illegal copies of our works in any form on the Internet, we would be grateful if you would provide us with the location address or website name. Please contact us at `copyright@packtpub.com` with a link to the material.

If you are interested in becoming an author: If there is a topic that you have expertise in and you are interested in either writing or contributing to a book, please visit `authors.packtpub.com`.

Reviews

Please leave a review. Once you have read and used this book, why not leave a review on the site that you purchased it from? Potential readers can then see and use your unbiased opinion to make purchase decisions, we at Packt can understand what you think about our products, and our authors can see your feedback on their book. Thank you!

For more information about Packt, please visit `packtpub.com`.

1
Introduction to Blockchain, Ethereum, and Smart Contracts

This decade has already seen the extraordinary evolution of the technology and computing ecosystem. Technological innovation and its impact has been noticeable across the spectrum, from the **Internet of Things (IoT)**, to **Artificial Intelligence (AI)**, to blockchains. Each of them has had a disruptive force within multiple industries and blockchains are one of the most disruptive technologies today. So much so that blockchains have the potential to change almost every industry. Blockchains are revolutionizing almost all industries and domains while bringing forward newer business models. Blockchains are not a new technology; however, they have gained momentum over the last couple of years. It is a big leap forward in terms of thinking about decentralized and distributed applications. It is about the current architectural landscape and strategies for moving toward immutable distributed databases.

In this first chapter, you will quickly learn and understand the basic and foundational concepts of blockchains and Ethereum. We will also discuss some of the important concepts that makes blockchains and Ethereum work. Also, we will touch briefly on the topic of smart contracts and how to author them using Solidity.

It is to be noted that this chapter briefly explains important blockchain concepts. It does not explain all concepts in detail and would require a complete book only for that purpose. Since Ethereum is an implementation of a blockchain, both the words have been used interchangeably in this book.

This chapter will focus on introducing the following topics:

- What is a blockchain and why is it used?
- Cryptography
- Ether and gas
- Blockchain and Ethereum architecture

- Nodes
- Mining
- Understanding accounts, transactions, and blocks
- Smart contracts

What is a blockchain?

A blockchain is essentially a decentralized distributed database or a ledger, as follows:

- **Decentralization:** In simple terms, it means that the application or service continues to be available and usable even if a server or a group of servers on a network crashes or is not available. The service or application is deployed on a network in a way that no server has absolute control over data and execution, rather each server has a current copy of data and execution logic.
- **Distributed:** This means that any server or node on a network is connected to every other node on the network. Rather than having one-to-one or one-to-many connectivity between servers, servers have many-to-many connections with other servers.
- **Database:** This refers to the location for storing durable data that can be accessed at any point in time. A database allows storage and retrieval of data as functionality and also provides management functionalities to manage data efficiently, such as export, import, backup, and restoration.
- **Ledger:** This is an accounting term. Think of it as specialized storage and retrieval of data. Think of ledgers that are available to banks. For example, when a transaction is executed with a bank—say, Tom deposits 100 dollars in his account, the bank enters this information in a ledger as a credit. At some point in the future Tom withdraws 25 dollars. The bank does not modify the existing entry and stored data from 100 to 75. Instead it adds another entry in the same ledger as a debit of 25 dollars. It means a ledger is a specialized database that does not allow modification of existing data. It allows you to create and append a new transaction to modify the current balance in the ledger. The blockchain is a database that has the same characteristics of a ledger. It allows newer transactions to be stored in an append-only pattern without any scope to modify past transactions. It is important here to understand that existing data can be modified by using a new transaction, but past transactions cannot be modified. A balance of 100 dollars can be modified at any time by executing a new debit or credit transaction, but previous transactions cannot be modified. Take a look at the following diagram for a better understanding:

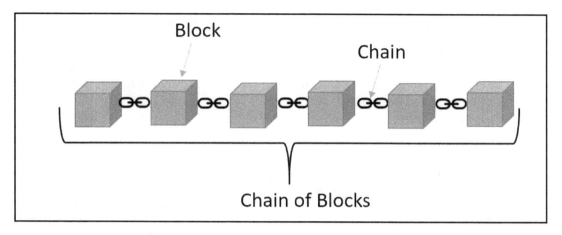

Blockchain means a chain of blocks. Blockchain means having multiple blocks chained together, with each block storing transactions in a way where it is not possible to change these transactions. We will discuss this in later sections when we talk about the storage of transactions and how immutability is achieved in a blockchain.

Because of being decentralized and distributed, blockchain solutions are stable, robust, durable, and highly available. There is no single point of failure. No single node or server is the owner of the data and solution, and everyone participates as a stakeholder.

Not being able to change and modify past transactions makes blockchain solutions highly trustworthy, transparent, and incorruptible.

Ethereum allows extending its functionality with the help of smart contracts. Smart contracts will be addressed in detail throughout this book.

Why blockchains?

The main objective of Ethereum is to accept transactions from accounts, update their state, and maintain this state as current till another transaction updates it again. The whole process of accepting, executing, and writing transactions can be divided into two phases in Ethereum. There is a decoupling between when a transaction is accepted by Ethereum and when the transaction is executed and written to the ledger. This decoupling is quite important for decentralization and distributed architecture to work as expected.

Blockchain helps primarily in the following three different ways:

- **Trust**: Blockchain helps in creating applications that are decentralized and collectively owned by multiple people. Nobody within this group has the power to change or delete previous transactions. Even if someone tries to do so, it will not be accepted by other stakeholders.
- **Autonomy**: There is no single owner for blockchain-based applications. No one controls the blockchain, but everyone participates in its activities. This helps in creating solutions that cannot be manipulated or induce corruption.
- **Intermediaries**: Blockchain-based applications can help remove the intermediaries from existing processes. Generally there is a central body, such as vehicle registration, license issuing, and so on, that acts as registrar for registering vehicles as well as issuing driver licenses. Without blockchain-based systems, there is no central body and if a license is issued or vehicle is registered after a blockchain mining process, that will remain a fact for an epoch time-period without the need of any central authority vouching for it.

Blockchain is heavily dependent on cryptography technologies as we discuss in the following section.

Cryptography

Cryptography is the science of converting plain simple text into secret, hidden, meaningful text, and vice-versa. It also helps in transmitting and storing data that cannot be easily deciphered using owned keys.

There are the following two types of cryptography in computing:

- Symmetric
- Asymmetric

Symmetric encryption and decryption

Symmetric cryptography refers to the process of using a single key for both encryption and decryption. It means the same key should be available to multiple people if they want to exchange messages using this form of cryptography.

Asymmetric encryption and decryption

Asymmetric cryptography refers to the process of using two keys for encryption and decryption. Any key can be used for encryption and decryption. Message encryption with a public key can be decrypted using a private key and messages encrypted by a private key can be decrypted using a public key. Let's understand this with the help of an example. Tom uses Alice's public key to encrypt messages and sends it to Alice. Alice can use her private key to decrypt the message and extract contents out of it. Messages encrypted with Alice's public key can only be decrypted by Alice as only she holds her private key and no one else. This is the general use case of asymmetric keys. There is another use which we will see while discussing digital signatures.

Hashing

Hashing is the process of transforming any input data into fixed length random character data, and it is not possible to regenerate or identify the original data from the resultant string data. Hashes are also known as fingerprint of input data. It is next to impossible to derive input data based on its hash value. Hashing ensures that even a slight change in input data will completely change the output data, and no one can ascertain the change in the original data. Another important property of hashing is that no matter the size of input string data, the length of its output is always fixed. For example, using the SHA256 hashing algorithm and function with any length of input will always generate 256 bit output data. This can especially become useful when large amounts of data can be stored as 256 bit output data. Ethereum uses the hashing technique quite extensively. It hashes every transaction, hashes the hash of two transactions at a time, and ultimately generates a single root transaction hash for every transaction within a block.

Another important property of hashing is that it is not mathematically feasible to identify two different input strings that will output the same hash. Similarly, it is not possible to computationally and mathematically find the input from the hash itself.

Ethereum used `Keccak256` as its hashing algorithm.

The following screenshot shows an example of hashing. The input `Ritesh Modi` generates a hash, as shown in the following screenshot:

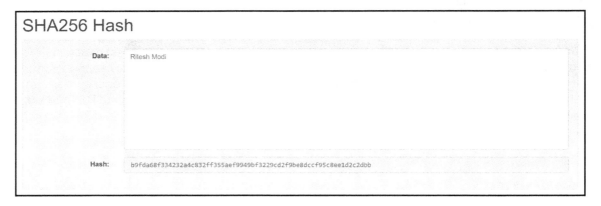

Even a small modification to input generates a completely different hash, as shown in the following screenshot:

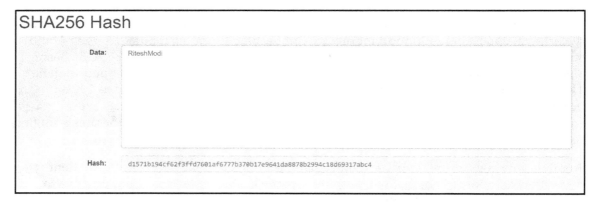

Digital signatures

Earlier, we discussed cryptography using asymmetric keys. One of the important cases for using asymmetric keys is in the creation and verification of a digital signature. Digital signatures are very similar to a signature done by an individual on a piece of paper. Similar to a paper signature, a digital signature helps in identifying an individual. It also helps in ensuring that messages are not tampered with in transit. Let's understand digital signatures with the help of an example.

Alice wants to send a message to Tom. How can Tom identify and ensure that the message has come from Alice only and that the message has not been changed or tampered with in transit? Instead of sending a raw message/transaction, Alice creates a hash of the entire payload and encrypts the hash with her private key. She appends the resultant digital signature to the hash and transmits it to Tom. When the transaction reaches Tom, he extracts the digital signature and decrypts it using Alice's public key to find the original hash. He also extracts the original hash from the rest of the message and compares both the hashes. If the hashes match, it means that it actually originated from Alice and that it has not been tampered with.

Digital signatures are used to sign transaction data by the owner of the asset or cryptocurrency, such as Ether.

Ether

Ether is the currency of Ethereum. Every activity on Ethereum that modifies its state costs Ether as a fee, and miners who are successful in generating and writing a block in a chain are also rewarded Ether. Ether can easily be converted to dollars or other traditional currencies through cryptoexchanges.

Ethereum has a metric system of denominations used as units of Ether. The smallest denomination or base unit of Ether is called **wei**. The following is a list of the named denominations and their value in wei which is available at https://github.com/ethereum/web3.js/blob/0.15.0/lib/utils/utils.js#L40:

```
var unitMap = {
    'wei' : '1'
    'kwei': '1000',
    'ada': '1000',
    'femtoether': '1000',
    'mwei': '1000000',
    'babbage': '1000000',
    'picoether': '1000000',
    'gwei': '1000000000',
    'shannon': '1000000000',
    'nanoether': '1000000000',
    'nano': '1000000000',
    'szabo': '1000000000000',
    'microether': '1000000000000',
    'micro': '1000000000000',
    'finney': '1000000000000000',
    'milliether': '1000000000000000',
    'milli': '1000000000000000',
```

```
    'ether': '1000000000000000000',
    'kether': '1000000000000000000000',
    'grand': '1000000000000000000000',
    'einstein': '1000000000000000000000',
    'mether': '1000000000000000000000000',
    'gether': '1000000000000000000000000000',
    'tether': '1000000000000000000000000000000'
};
```

Gas

In the previous section, it was mentioned that fees are paid using Ether for any execution that changes state in Ethereum. Ether is traded on public exchanges and its price fluctuates daily. If Ether is used for paying fees, then the cost of using the same service could be very high on certain days and low on other days. People will wait for the price of Ether to fall to execute their transactions. This is not ideal for a platform such as Ethereum. Gas helps in alleviating this problem. Gas is the internal currency of Ethereum. The execution and resource utilization cost is predetermined in Ethereum in terms of gas units. This is also known as **gas cost**. There is also **gas price** that can be adjusted to a lower price when the price of Ether increases and a higher price when the price of Ether decreases. For example, to invoke a function in a contract that modifies a string will cost gas, which is predetermined, and users should pay in terms of gas to ensure smooth execution of this transaction.

Blockchain and Ethereum architecture

Blockchain is an architecture comprising multiple components and what makes blockchain unique is the way these components function and interact with each other. Some of the important Ethereum components are **Ethereum Virtual Machine (EVM)**, miner, block, transaction, consensus algorithm, account, smart contract, mining, Ether, and gas. We are going to discuss each of these components in this chapter.

A blockchain network consists of multiple nodes belonging to miners and some nodes that do not mine but help in execution of smart contracts and transactions. These are known as EVMs. Each node is connected to another node on the network. These nodes use peer-to-peer protocol to talk to each other. They, by default, use port 30303 to talk among themselves.

Each miner maintains an instance of ledger. A ledger contains all blocks in the chain. With multiple miners it is quite possible that each miner's ledger instance might have different blocks to another. The miners synchronize their blocks on an on-going basis to ensure that every miner's ledger instance is the same as the other.

Details about ledgers, blocks, and transactions are discussed in detail in subsequent sections in this chapter.

The EVM also hosts smart contracts. Smart contracts help in extending Ethereum by writing custom business functionality into it. These smart contracts can be executed as part of a transaction and it follows the process of mining as discussed earlier.

A person having an account on a network can send a message for transfer of Ether from their account to another or can send a message to invoke a function within a contract. Ethereum does not distinguish them as far as transactions are considered. The transaction must be digitally signed with an account holder's private key. This is to ensure that the identity of the sender can be established while verifying the transaction and changing the balances of multiple accounts. Let's take a look at the components of Ethereum in the following diagram:

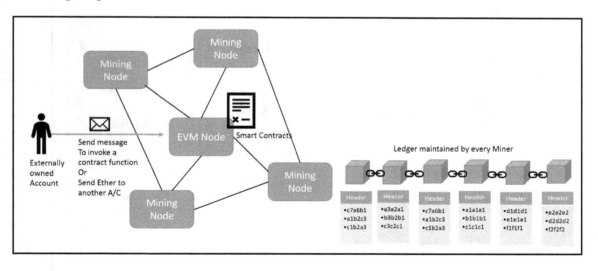

How are blocks related to each other?

In blockchain and Ethereum every block is related to another block. There is a parent-child relationship between two blocks. There can be only one child to a parent and a child can have a single parent. This helps in forming a chain in blockchain. Blocks are explained in a later section in this chapter. In the following diagram, three blocks are shown—**Block 1**, **Block 2**, and **Block 3**. **Block 1** is the parent of **Block 2** and **Block 2** is the parent of **Block 3**. The relationship is established by storing the parent block's hash in a child's block header. **Block 2** stores the hash of **Block 1** in its header and **Block 3** stored the hash of **Block 2** in its header. So, the question arises—who is the parent of the first block? Ethereum has a concept of the **genesis block** also known as **first block**. This block is created automatically when the chain is first initiated. You can say that a chain is initiated with the first block known as the **Genesis Block** and the formation of this block is driven through the `genesis.json` file. Let's take a look at the following diagram:

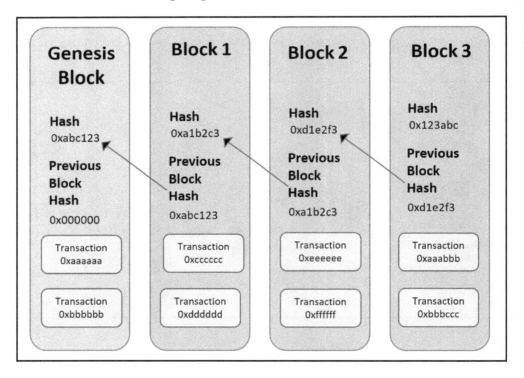

The following chapter will show how to use the `genesis.json` file to create the first block while initializing the blockchain.

How are transactions and blocks related to each other?

Now that we know that blocks are related to each other, you will be interested in knowing how transactions are related to blocks. Ethereum stores transactions within blocks. Each block has an upper gas limit and each transaction needs a certain amount of gas to be consumed as part of its execution. The cumulative gas from all transactions that are not yet written in a ledger cannot surpass the block gas limit. This ensures that all transactions do not get stored within a single block. As soon as the gas limit is reached, other transactions are removed from the block and mining begins thereafter.

The transactions are hashed and stored in the block. The hashes of two transactions are taken and hashed further to generate another hash. This process eventually provides a single hash from all transactions stored within the block. This hash is known as the **transaction Merkle root hash** and is stored in a block's header. A change in any transaction will result in a change in its hash and, eventually, a change in the root transaction hash. It will have a cumulative effect because the hash of the block will change, and the child block has to change its hash because it stores its parent hash. This helps in making transactions immutable. This is also shown in the following diagram:

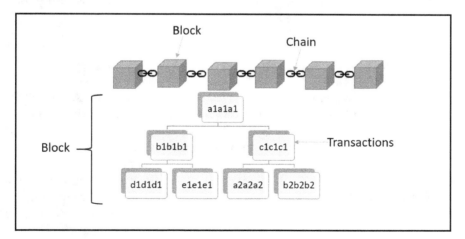

Ethereum nodes

Nodes represent the computers that are connected using a peer-to-peer protocol to form an Ethereum network.

There are the following two types of nodes in Ethereum:

- EVM
- Mining nodes

It is to be noted that this distinction is made to clarify concepts of Ethereum. In most scenarios, there is no dedicated EVM. Instead, all nodes act as miners as well as EVM nodes.

EVM

Think of EVM as the execution runtime for an Ethereum network. EVMs are primarily responsible for providing a runtime that can execute code written in smart contracts. It can access accounts, both contract and externally owned, and its own storage data. It does not have access to the overall ledger but does have limited information about the current transaction.

EVMs are the execution components in Ethereum. The purpose of an EVM is to execute the code in a smart contract line by line. However, when a transaction is submitted, the transaction is not executed immediately. Instead it is pooled in a transaction pool. These transactions are not yet written to the Ethereum ledger.

Ethereum mining nodes

A miner is responsible for writing transactions to the Ethereum chain. A miner's job is very similar to that of an accountant. As an accountant is responsible for writing and maintaining the ledger; similarly, a miner is solely responsible for writing a transaction to an Ethereum ledger. A miner is interested in writing transactions to a ledger because of the reward associated with it. Miners get two types of reward—a reward for writing a block to the chain and cumulative gas fees from all transactions in the block. There are generally many miners available within a blockchain network each trying and competing to write transactions. However, only one miner can write the block to the ledger and the rest will not be able to write the current block.

The miner responsible for writing the block is determined by way of a puzzle. The challenge is given to every miner and they try to solve the puzzle using their compute power. The miner who solves the puzzle first writes the block containing transactions to his own ledger and sends the block and nonce value to other miners for verification. Once verified and accepted, the new block is written to all ledgers belonging to miners. In this process, the winning miner also receives 5 Ether as reward. Every mining node maintains its own instance of the Ethereum ledger and the ledger is ultimately the same across all miners. It is the miner's job to ensure that their ledger is updated with the latest blocks. Following are the three important functions performed by miners or mining nodes:

- Mine or create a new block with a transaction and write the same to the Ethereum ledger
- Advertise and send a newly mined block to other miners
- Accept new blocks mined by other miners and keep its own ledger instance up-to-date

Mining nodes refer to the nodes that belong to miners. These nodes are part of the same network where the EVM is hosted. At some point in time, the miners will create a new block, collect all transactions from the transaction pool, and add them to the newly created block. Finally, this block is added to the chain. There are additional concepts such as consensus and solving of target puzzle before writing the block that will be explained in the following section.

How does mining work?

The process of mining explained here is applicable to every miner on the network and every miner keeps executing the tasks mentioned here regularly.

Miners are always looking forward to mining new blocks, and are also listening actively to receive new blocks from other miners. They are also listening for new transactions to store in the transaction pool. Miners also spread the incoming transactions to other connected nodes after validation. As mentioned before, at some point, the miner collects all transactions from the transaction pool. This activity is done by all miners.

The miner constructs a new block and adds all transactions to it. Before adding these transactions, it will check if any of the transactions are not already written in a block that it might receive from other miners. If so, it will discard those transactions.

The miner will add their own coinbase transaction for getting rewards for mining the block.

The next task for a miner is to generate the block header and perform the following tasks:

1. The miner takes hashes of two transactions at a time to generate a new hash till he gets a single hash from all transactions. The hash is referred to as a **root** transaction hash or Merkle root transaction hash. This hash is added to the block header.
2. The miner also identifies the hash of the previous block. The previous block will become parent to the current block and its hash will also be added to the block header.
3. The miner calculates the state and receipts of transaction root hashes and adds them to the block header.
4. A nonce and timestamp is also added to the block header.
5. A block hash consisting of both block header and body is generated.
6. The mining process starts where the miner keeps changing the nonce value and tries to find a hash that will satisfy as an answer to the given puzzle. It is to be kept in mind that everything mentioned here is executed by every miner in the network.
7. Eventually, one of the miners will be able to solve the puzzle and advertise the same to other miners in the network. The other miners will verify the answer and, if found correct, will further verify every transaction, accept the block, and append the same to their ledger instance.

This entire process is also known as **Proof of Work** (**PoW**) wherein a miner provides proof that it is has worked on computing the final answer that could satisfy as solution to the puzzle. There are other algorithms such as **Proof of Stake** (**PoS**) and **Proof of Authority** (**PoA**), but they are not used or discussed in this book.

The header block and its content is shown in the following diagram:

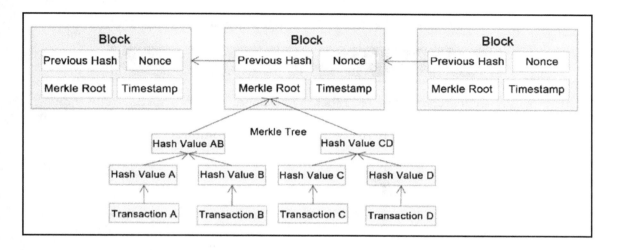

Ethereum accounts

Accounts are the main building blocks for the Ethereum ecosystem. It is an interaction between accounts that Ethereum wants to store as transactions in its ledger. There are two types of accounts available in Ethereum—externally owned accounts and contract accounts. Each account, by default, has a property named balance that helps in querying the current balance of Ether.

Externally owned accounts

Externally owned accounts are accounts that are owned by people on Ethereum. Accounts are not referred to by name in Ethereum. When an externally owned account is created on Ethereum by an individual, a public/private key is generated. The private key is kept safe with the individual while the public key becomes the identity of this externally owned account. This public key is generally of 256 characters, however, Ethereum uses the first 160 characters to represent the identity of an account.

If Bob, for example, creates an account on an Ethereum network—whether private or public, he will have his private key available to himself while the first 160 characters of his public key will become his identity. Other accounts on the network can then send Ether or other cryptocurrencies based on Ether to this account.

An account on Ethereum looks like the one shown in the following screenshot:

```
0xa57de277ede9c1521f51f6989ed2497a5b9c1926
```

An externally owned account can hold Ether in its balance and does not have any code associated with it. It can execute transactions with other externally owned accounts and it can also execute transactions by invoking functions within contracts.

Contract accounts

Contract accounts are very similar to externally owned accounts. They are identified using their public address. They do not have a private key. They can hold Ether similar to externally owned accounts; however, they contain code—code for smart contracts consisting of functions and state variables.

Transactions

A transaction is an agreement between a buyer and a seller, a supplier and a consumer, or a provider and a consumer that there will be an exchange of assets, products, or services for currency, cryptocurrency, or some other asset, either in the present or in the future. Ethereum helps in executing the transaction. Following are the three types of transactions that can be executed in Ethereum:

- **Transfer of Ether from one account to another**: The accounts can be externally owned accounts or contract accounts. Following are the possible cases:
  - An externally owned account sending Ether to another externally owned account in a transaction
  - An externally owned account sending Ether to a contract account in a transaction
  - A contract account sending Ether to another contract account in a transaction
  - A contract account sending Ether to an externally owned account in a transaction

- **Deployment of a smart contract**: An externally owned account can deploy a contract using a transaction in EVM.
- **Using or invoking a function within a contract**: Executing a function in a contract that changes state is considered a transaction in Ethereum. If executing a function does not change a state, it does not require a transaction.

A transaction has some of the following important properties related to it:

- The `from` account property denotes the account that is originating the transaction and represents an account that is ready to send some gas or Ether. Both gas and Ether concepts were discussed earlier in this chapter. The `from` account can be externally owned or a contract account.
- The `to` account property refers to an account that is receiving Ether or benefits in lieu of an exchange. For transactions related to deployment of contract, the `to` field is empty. It can be externally owned or a contract account.
- The `value` account property refers to the amount of Ether that is transferred from one account to another.
- The `input` account property refers to the compiled contract bytecode and is used during contract deployment in EVM. It is also used for storing data related to smart contract function calls along with its parameters. A typical transaction in Ethereum where a contract function is invoked is shown here. In the following screenshot, notice the `input` field containing the function call to contract along with its parameters:

```
{ blockHash: '0xba93a91df520c7565e80347346e47b83a41d473a33352d1cf7e689c30b305ba5',
  blockNumber: 70,
  from: '0xa57de277ede9c1521f51f6989ed2497a5b9c1926',
  gas: 90000,
  gasPrice: BigNumber { s: 1, e: 10, c: [ 18000000000 ] },
  hash: '0x6b65b86462e6aa89d5f9469ce03b9ea21e8bf72f8c11aa72de2978f9b7a5b9fd',
  input: '0xc8aaea4000000000000000000000000000000000000000000000000000000000000000000200000000000000000000000000000000
  nonce: 1,
  to: '0x6b90c690b23af11c9575c2b9b8e26d47d84b4f8b',
  transactionIndex: 0,
  value: BigNumber { s: 1, e: 0, c: [ 0 ] },
  v: '0x42',
  r: '0xd4f5adb0f1739105668afa5aba700ae4f031e88e9f21bdb7ac787a3af156baf7',
  s: '0x7f89cda2ae325948f73bcd8da93e2cd6cf9917b22e32d93c3f8caedc0edcd1' }
```

- The `blockHash` account property refers to the hash of block to which this transaction belongs.
- The `blockNumber` account property is the block in which this transaction belongs.

- The `gas` account property refers to the amount of gas supplied by the sender who is executing this transaction.
- The `gasPrice` account property refers to the price per gas the sender was willing to pay in wei (we have already learned about wei in the *Ether* section in this chapter). Total gas is computed at *gas units * gas price*.
- The `hash` account property refers to the hash of the transaction.
- The `nonce` account property refers to the number of transactions made by the sender prior to the current transaction.
- The `transactionIndex` account property refers to the serial number of the current transactions in the block.
- The `value` account property refers to the amount of Ether transferred in wei.
- The `v`, `r`, and `s` account properties relate to digital signatures and the signing of the transaction.

A typical transaction in Ethereum, where an externally owned account sends some Ether to another externally owned account, is shown here. Notice the `input` field is not used here. Since two Ethers were sent in transaction, the `value` field is showing the value accordingly in wei as shown in the following screenshot:

```
{ blockHash: '0x78ddc6d1d18a52811888dea659a69f35f424aa0ec48562b956d3524e80fcf893',
  blockNumber: 105,
  from: '0xa57de277ede9c1521f51f6989ed2497a5b9c1926',
  gas: 90000,
  gasPrice: BigNumber { s: 1, e: 10, c: [ 18000000000 ] },
  hash: '0x93768f05999d54edde1982f82150b429b3cba0014233defab34701e6b6a7ec87',
  input: '0x',
  nonce: 2,
  to: '0x9d2a327b320da739ed6b0da33c3809946cc8cf6a',
  transactionIndex: 0,
  value: BigNumber { s: 1, e: 18, c: [ 20000 ] },
  v: '0x41',
  r: '0x9efb14382840ab5fcdf2d33f32638e895beb9cee35d4d79675c183c7fddef8f5',
  s: '0x658bac95226e3a8a90d497ce8c841e0833c01b5a2567bb8c2aa126ba95e1fbd2' }
```

One method to send Ether from an externally owned account to another externally owned account is shown in the following code snippet using `web3` JavaScript framework, which will be covered later in this book:

```
web.eth.sendTransaction({from: web.eth.accounts[0], to:
"0x9d2a327b320da739ed6b0da33c3809946cc8cf6a", value: web.toWei(2,
'ether')})
```

A typical transaction in Ethereum where a contract is deployed is shown in the following screenshot. In the following screenshot, notice the `input` field containing the bytecode of contract:

```
{ blockHash: '0x041cdd69390b130e0b54c53f2afb46d79a06708dcf8414aa1ba4bbb40a2786b7',
  blockNumber: 6,
  from: '0xa57de277ede9c1521f51f6989ed2497a5b9c1926',
  gas: 1000000,
  gasPrice: BigNumber { s: 1, e: 10, c: [ 18000000000 ] },
  hash: '0x6f5a74e5191f745d0e38fa67841ba6b36cf03a7c0fd7729ef355fe77c86487a2',
  input: '0x60606040523415610000f57600080fd5b6102c38061001e6000396000f300606060405260043610610004b5763ffffffff7c0100
561005b57600080fd5b61006361012d565b60405160208082528190810183818151181526020019150805190602001908083836005b8381101
0191505b50925050506040518091039f35b34156100e557600080fd5b61012b6004602481358181019083013586020601f820181900484102
615610100020316600290048601f0160208091040260200160405190810160405280929190818152602001828054600181600116156101000
0190602001808311610ae57829003601f168201915b505050505090505b90565b60008180516101e9929160200190610ff565b5050565b60
1024057805160ff191683800117855561026d565b828001600101855582156102 6d579182015b8281111561026d5782518255916020019190
77752e38ed74bb682568cb64c68f24734ab95e18740deee526b95eff79e40029',
  nonce: 0,
  to: null,
  transactionIndex: 0,
  value: BigNumber { s: 1, e: 0, c: [ 0 ] },
  v: '0x42',
  r: '0x29887013743c6fc9a4bb78c6d3ca2974eac6f41b21d2d0bb6fdfe09b71202602',
  s: '0xaaa9366553495c9c81ecb9806d0cdcb4e0ed5d688797be099978e260ae53e34' }
```

Blocks

Blocks are an important concept in Ethereum. Blocks are containers for a transaction. A block contains multiple transactions. Each block has a different number of transactions based on gas limit and block size. Gas limit will be explained in detail in later sections. The blocks are chained together to form a blockchain. Each block has a parent block and it stores the hash of the parent block in its header. Only the first block, known as the genesis block, does not have a parent.

A typical block in Ethereum is shown in the following screenshot:

```
{ difficulty: BigNumber { s: 1, e: 5, c: [ 135070 ] },
  extraData: '0xd7830107028467657468856576f312e398777696e646f7773',
  gasLimit: 4011042861,
  gasUsed: 43406,
  hash: '0xba93a91df520c7565e80347346e47b83a41d473a33352d1cf7e689c30b305ba5',
  logsBloom: '0x000000000000000000000000000000000000000000000000000000000000000000000000000000000
0000000000000000000000000000000000000000000000000000000000000000000000000000000000000000000000000000000000
000000000000000000000000000000000000000000000000000000',
  miner: '0xa57de277ede9c1521f51f6989ed2497a5b9c1926',
  mixHash: '0x4e80de770c329aebbc2e9e861190784f57b7f9910bbb049534828052284f32e4',
  nonce: '0x655dee191333922c',
  number: 70,
  parentHash: '0x27d3dbc34614f88583f29ea1b7546e83563e55638b1d0a258de04f4912f42aaf',
  receiptsRoot: '0x5dff465dd8fc4ad02c71ec4099284ecaf91ed9bb600f7903978386059c16fb8d',
  sha3Uncles: '0x1dcc4de8dec75d7aab85b567b6ccd41ad312451b948a7413f0a142fd40d49347',
  size: 742,
  stateRoot: '0xb15363a8958d218eff295b5e877517ee4243f1b681d987793c5ec30a04bc4592',
  timestamp: 1511421241,
  totalDifficulty: BigNumber { s: 1, e: 6, c: [ 9302609 ] },
  transactions:
   [ '0x6b65b86462e6aa89d5f9469ce03b9ea21e8bf72f8c11aa72de2978f9b7a5b9fd' ],
  transactionsRoot: '0x5aceca068d1a7ac8d8ecd8f19469ec7c687cb6ceed54e0db39b58dfdf6481de9',
  uncles: [] }
```

There are a lot of properties associated with a block, providing insights and metadata about it, and following are some of important properties along with their descriptions:

- The `difficulty` property determines the complexity of the puzzle/challenge given to miners for this block.
- The `gasLimit` property determines the maximum gas allowed. This helps in determining how many transactions can be part of the block.
- The `gasUsed` property refers to the actual gas used for this block for executing all transactions in it.
- The `hash` property refers to the hash of the block.
- The `nonce` property refers to the number that helps in solving the challenge.
- The `miner` property is the account identifier of the miner, also known as coinbase or etherbase.
- The `number` property is the sequential number of this block on the chain.
- The `parentHash` property refers to the parent block's hash.
- The `receiptsRoot`, `stateRoot`, and `transactionsRoot` properties refer to Merkle trees discussed during the mining process.
- The `transactions` property refers to an array of transactions that are part of this block.
- The `totalDifficulty` property refers to the total difficulty of the chain.

An end-to-end transaction

Armed with the understanding of the foundational concepts of blockchain and Ethereum, it's time to see a complete end-to-end transaction and how it flows through multiple components and gets stored in the ledger.

In this example, Sam wants to send a digital asset (for example, dollars) to Mark. Sam generates a transaction message containing the `from`, `to`, and `value` fields and sends it across to the Ethereum network. The transaction is not written to the ledger immediately and instead is placed in a transaction pool.

The mining node creates a new block and takes all transactions from the pool honoring the gas limit criteria and adds them to the block. This activity is done by all miners on the network. Sam's transaction will also be a part of this process.

The miners compete trying to solve the challenge thrown to them. The winner is the miner who can solve the challenge first. After a period (of seconds) one of the miners will advertise that they has found the solution to the challenge and that they are the winner and should write the block to the chain. The winner sends the challenge solution along with the new block to all other miners. The rest of the miners validate and verify the solution and, once satisfied that the solution is indeed correct and that the original miner has cracked the challenge, they accept the new block containing Sam's transaction to append in their instance of the ledger. This generates a new block on the chain that is persisted across time and space. During this time, the accounts of both parties are updated with the new balance. Finally, the block is replicated across every node in the network.

The preceding example can be well understood with the following diagram:

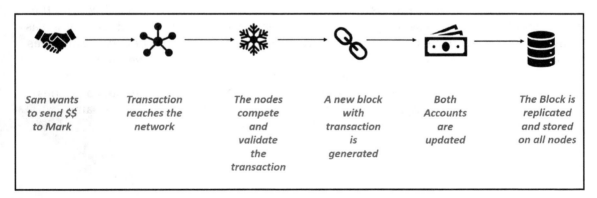

| Sam wants to send $$ to Mark | Transaction reaches the network | The nodes compete and validate the transaction | A new block with transaction is generated | Both Accounts are updated | The Block is replicated and stored on all nodes |

What is a contract?

A contract is a legal document that binds two or more parties who agree to execute a transaction immediately or in the future. Since contracts are legal documents, they are enforced and implemented by law. Examples of contracts are an individual entering into a contract with an insurance company for covering their health insurance, an individual buying a piece of land from another individual, or a company selling its shares to another company.

What is a smart contract?

A smart contract is custom logic and code deployed and executed within an Ethereum virtual environment. Smart contracts are digitized and codified rules of transaction between accounts. Smart contracts help in transferring digital assets between accounts as an atomic transaction. Smart contracts can store data. The data stored can be used to record information, facts, associations, balances, and any other information needed to implement logic for real-world contracts. Smart contracts are very similar to object-oriented classes. A smart contract can call another smart contract just like an object-oriented object can create and use objects of another class. Think of smart contracts as a small program consisting of functions. You can create an instance of the contract and invoke functions to view and update contract data along with the execution of some logic.

How to write smart contracts?

There are multiple smart contracts authoring tools including Visual Studio. However, the easiest and fastest way to develop smart contracts is to use a browser-based tool known as **Remix**. Remix is available on `http://remix.ethereum.org`. Remix is a new name and was earlier known as **browser-solidity**. Remix provides a rich integrated development environment in a browser for authoring, developing, deploying, and troubleshooting contracts written using the Solidity language. All contract management related activities such as authoring, deploying, and troubleshooting can be performed from the same environment without moving to other windows or tabs.

Not everyone is comfortable using the online version of Remix to author their smart contracts. Remix is an open source tool that can be downloaded from `https://github.com/ethereum/browser-Solidity` and compiled to run a private version on a local computer. Another advantage of running Remix locally is that it can connect to local private chain networks directly; otherwise, users will first have to author the contract online and then copy the same to a file, compile, and deploy manually to a private network. Let's explore Remix by performing the following steps:

1. Navigate to `remix.ethereum.org` and the site will open in a browser with a default contract as shown in the following screenshot. If you do not need this contract, it can be deleted:

```
« ±    browser/ballot.sol  ×                                                »
  1  pragma solidity ^0.4.0;
  2 ▾ contract Ballot {
  3
  4 ▾     struct Voter {
  5            uint weight;
  6            bool voted;
  7            uint8 vote;
  8            address delegate;
  9        }
 10 ▾     struct Proposal {
 11            uint voteCount;
 12        }
 13
 14        address chairperson;
 15        mapping(address => Voter) voters;
 16        Proposal[] proposals;
 17
 18        /// Create a new ballot with $(_numProposals) different proposals.
 19 ▾     function Ballot(uint8 _numProposals) public {
 20            chairperson = msg.sender;
 21            voters[chairperson].weight = 1;
 22            proposals.length = _numProposals;
 23        }
 24
 25        /// Give $(toVoter) the right to vote on this ballot.
 26        /// May only be called by $(chairperson).
 27 ▾     function giveRightToVote(address toVoter) public {
 28            if (msg.sender != chairperson || voters[toVoter].voted) return;
 29            voters[toVoter].weight = 1;
 30        }
 31

 ⌄  ⦸   [2] only remix transactions, script ▾    Q  Search transactions        ☐ Listen on network
```

2. The first thing we need to do is to create a new contract by selecting + from Remix's left menu bar.

3. Then, provide a name for a new Solidity file that has an extension .sol. Name the contract HelloWorld and click on **OK** to continue as shown in the following screenshot. This will create a blank contract:

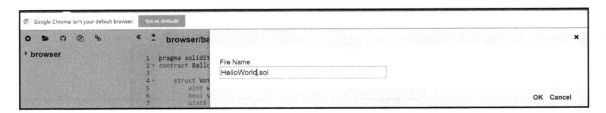

4. Type the following code in the empty authoring pane to create your first contract. This contract will be explained in detail in Chapter 3, *Introducing Solidity*. For now, it is sufficient to understand that the contract is created using the contract keyword; you can declare global state variables and functions; and contracts are saved with the .sol file extension. In the following code snippet, the HelloWorld contracts returns the HelloWorld string when the GetHelloWorld function is called:

```
pragma Solidity ^0.4.18;
contract HelloWorld
{
string private stateVariable = "Hello World";
function GetHelloWorld() public view returns (string)
{
return stateVariable;
}
}
```

Look at the action window to the right of Remix. It has got several tabs—**Compile**, **Run**, **Settings**, **Debugger**, **Analysis**, and **Support**. These action tabs help in compiling, deploying, troubleshooting, and invoking contracts. The **Compile** tab compiles the contract into bytecode—code that is understood by Ethereum. It displays warnings and errors as you author and edit the contract. These warnings and errors are to be taken seriously and they really help in creating robust contracts. The **Run** tab is the place where you will spend the most time, apart from writing the contract. Remix comes bundled with the Ethereum runtime within the browser. The **Run** tab allows you to deploy the contract to this runtime using the **JavaScript VM** environment in the **Environment** option. The **Injected Web3** environment is used along with tools such as Mist and MetaMask, which will be covered in the next chapter, and **Web3 Provider** can be used when using Remix in a local environment connecting to private network. In our case for this chapter, the default, **JavaScript VM** is sufficient. The rest of the options will be discussed later in `Chapter 3`, *Introducing Solidity*.

5. However, the important action is deployment of a contract and that can be done using the **Create** button to deploy the contract that is shown in the following screenshot:

```
browser/HelloWorld.sol
1    pragma solidity ^0.4.18;
2
3    contract HelloWorld
4  ▾ {
5
6        string private stateVariable   = "Hello World";
7
8  ▾     function  GetHelloWorld() public view returns (string){
9            return stateVariable;
10
11       }
12   }
```

6. Click on the **Create** button to deploy the contract to the **browser** Ethereum runtime and this will list all the functions available within the contract below the **Create** button. Since we only had a single function `GetHelloWorld`, the same is displayed as shown in the following screenshot:

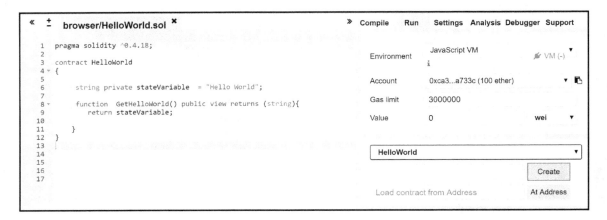

7. Click on the **GetHelloWorld** button to invoke and execute the function. The lower pane of Remix will show the results of execution as shown in the following screenshot:

Congratulations, you have created, deployed, and also executed a function on your first contract. The code for the `HelloWorld` contract is accompanied with this chapter and can be used in Remix if you are not interested in typing the contract.

How are contracts deployed?

Remix makes deployment of contracts a breeze; however, it is performing a lot of steps behind the scenes. It is always useful to understand the process of deploying contracts to have finer control over the deployment process.

The first step is the compilation of contracts. The compilation is done using the Solidity compiler. The next chapter will show you how to download and compile a contract using the Solidity compiler.

The compiler generates the following two major artifacts:

- ABI definition
- Contracts bytecode

Think of the **Application Binary Interface** (**ABI**) as an interface consisting of all external and public function declarations along with their parameters and return types. The ABI defines the contract and any caller wanting to invoke any contract function can use the ABI to do so.

The bytecode is what represents the contract and it is deployed in the Ethereum ecosystem. The bytecode is required during deployment and ABI is needed for invoking functions in a contract.

A new instance of a contract is created using the ABI definition.

Deploying a contract itself is a transaction. A transaction is created for deploying the contract on Ethereum. The bytecode and ABI are necessary inputs for deploying a contract.

As any transaction execution costs gas in Euthereum, appropriate quantity of gas should be supplied while deploying the contract. As and when the transaction is mined, the contract is would be available for interaction through contract address.

Using the newly generated address, callers can invoke functions within the contract.

Summary

This chapter was an introduction to blockchains and, more specifically, to Ethereum. Having a good understanding of the big picture about how blockchains and Ethereum work will go a long way in understanding how to write robust, secure, and cost effective smart contracts using Solidity. This chapter covered the basics of blockchain, explained what blockchains are, why blockchains are important, and how they help in building decentralized and distributed applications. The architecture of Ethereum was discussed in brief along with some of the important concepts such as transactions, blocks, gas, Ether, accounts, cryptography, and mining. This chapter also touched briefly on the topic of smart contracts, using Remix to author smart contracts and how to execute them using Remix itself. I've kept this chapter brief since the rest of the book will explain these concepts further and it will allow you to quickly develop Solidity-based smart contracts.

You'll notice that this chapter does not contain any mention of Ethereum tools and utilities. This is what we will cover in the next chapter, by diving straight in and installing Ethereum and its toolset. The Ethereum ecosystem is quite rich and there are lots of tools. We will cover important ones, such as `web3.js`, TestRPC, Geth, Mist, and MetaMask.

Installing Ethereum and Solidity 2

In the previous chapter, we had an overview of all major concepts related to blockchains, particularly focusing on ones related to Ethereum and discussed the fundamentals related to working with blockchains in general. Ethereum-based blockchain solutions can be deployed to multiple networks. They can be deployed on public networks, test networks, or private networks. This chapter focuses on introducing and deploying Ethereum-based tools and utilities that are needed for building Ethereum-based solutions. There are plenty of tools in the Ethereum ecosystem and this chapter will focus on some of the most important and necessary tools. The tools will be deployed on Windows Server 2016 on Azure Cloud. However, they can be deployed on Linux, Mac, and any virtual machine or physical computer, as well. This will also be used as our development environment for testing, deploying, creating, and using Solidity contracts throughout this book.

In this chapter, we'll cover the following topics:

- Introducing Ethereum networks
- Installing and configuring Geth
- Creating a private network
- Installing and configuring TestRPC
- Installing Solidity compiler—solc
- Installing web3 framework
- Installing and working with Mist
- Installing and working with MetaMask

Ethereum networks

Ethereum is an open source platform for creating and deploying distributed applications.

Ethereum is backed up by a large number of computers (also known as nodes)—all interconnected and storing data in a distributed ledger. Distributed ledger here means that a copy of this ledger is available to each and every node on the network. It provides flexibility to its developers to deploy their solution to multiple types. Developers should choose an appropriate network based on their requirements and use cases. These different networks also help in deploying solutions and smart contracts on networks that do not actually cost any Ether or money. There are networks that are free of cost while there are ones that require its users to pay in terms of Ether or other currencies for its usage.

Main network

The main Ethereum network is a global public network that anybody can use. It can be accessed using an account and everybody is free to create an account and deploy their solutions and smart contracts. Using a main network incurs costs in terms of gas. The main network is known as **Homestead** and was earlier known as **Frontier**. This is a public chain accessible over the internet and anybody can connect to it and access both data and transactions stored in it.

Test network

A **test network** exists to help facilitate and increase adoption of the Ethereum blockchain. They are the exact replica of the main network. Using these networks does not cost anything for deployment and usage of contracts. They are completely free of cost. This is because test Ethers can be generated using faucets and used on these networks. There are multiple test networks available at the time of writing, such as Ropsten, Kovan, and Rinkeby.

Ropsten

Ropsten is one of the first test networks that use PoW consensus methods for generating blocks. It was earlier known as **Morden**. As mentioned before, it is completely free of cost for usage and it can be used during the building and testing of smart contracts. It can be used by using the `--testnet` option available in Geth. Geth will be explained in detail in the next section. This is by far the most popular test network.

Rinkeby

Rinkeby is another Ethereum-based test network that uses PoA as its consensus mechanism. PoW and PoA are different mechanisms for building consensus among miners. PoW is robust enough to maintain immutability and decentralization of data; however, it has drawbacks in not having enough control over miners. PoA, on the other hand, has all the benefits of PoW along with having more control over the miners.

Kovan

Kovan test networks can only be used by parity clients and hence won't be discussed or used in this book. However more information is available at `https://kovan-testnet.github.io/website/`.

Private network

A **private** network is created and hosted on a private infrastructure. Private networks are controlled by a single organization and they have full control over it. There are solutions, contracts, and use cases that an organization might not want to put on a public network even for test purposes. They want to use private chains for development, testing, and production environments. Organizations should create and host a private network and they will have full control over it. Further in this chapter, we will see how to create your own private network.

Consortium network

A **consortium** network is also a private network, however, with a difference. The consortium network comprises nodes, each managed by a different organization. In effect, no organization has a control over the data and chain. However, it is shared within the organization and everyone from these organizations can view and modify the current state. These might be accessible through the internet or completely private networks using VPN.

Geth

Implementation of Ethereum nodes and clients is available in multiple languages, including Go, C++, Python, JavaScript, Java, Ruby, and more. The functionality or usability of these clients are the same across languages, and developers should choose an implementation they are most comfortable with. This book uses the Go implementation known as Geth, which acts as an Ethereum client to connect to public and test networks. It is also used to create the mining and EVM (transaction nodes) for private networks. Geth is a command-line tool written in Go for creating a node and miners on a private chain. It can be installed on Windows, Linux, and Mac as well. Now, its time to install Geth.

Installing Geth on Windows

The first step in creating a private Ethereum network is to download and install Geth (**go-ethereum**) tool.

In this section, the steps to download and install Geth on Windows are as follows:

1. Geth can be downloaded from the `https://ethereum.github.io/go-ethereum/downloads/` page. It is available for both 32 and 64 bit machines. Windows Server 2016 on Azure is used for all purposes in this book.
2. After downloading, start the installation process by executing the executable and follow the steps, accepting the defaults. Install development tools as a recommended practice on development environments.
3. Once Geth is installed, it should be available from Command Prompt or PowerShell.
4. Open Command Prompt and type `geth -help`.

 A word of caution here—just typing Geth and executing it will connect Geth to a public main network and it will start syncing and downloading all the blocks and transactions.

The current chain has more than 30 GB of data. `help` will show all the commands and options available with Geth. It will also show the current version as shown in the following screenshot:

```
Administrator: Command Prompt
Microsoft Windows [Version 10.0.14393]
(c) 2016 Microsoft Corporation. All rights reserved.

C:\Users\citynextadmin>geth help
NAME:
   geth - the go-ethereum command line interface

   Copyright 2013-2017 The go-ethereum Authors

USAGE:
   geth [options] command [command options] [arguments...]

VERSION:
   1.7.2-stable-1db4ecdc

COMMANDS:
    account      Manage accounts
    attach       Start an interactive JavaScript environment (connect to node)
    bug          opens a window to report a bug on the geth repo
    console      Start an interactive JavaScript environment
    copydb       Create a local chain from a target chaindata folder
    dump         Dump a specific block from storage
    dumpconfig   Show configuration values
    export       Export blockchain into file
    import       Import a blockchain file
    init         Bootstrap and initialize a new genesis block
    js           Execute the specified JavaScript files
    license      Display license information
    makecache    Generate ethash verification cache (for testing)
    makedag      Generate ethash mining DAG (for testing)
    monitor      Monitor and visualize node metrics
    removedb     Remove blockchain and state databases
    version      Print version numbers
    wallet       Manage Ethereum presale wallets
    help, h      Shows a list of commands or help for one command
```

Geth is based on JSON RPC protocol. It defines the specification for remote procedure calls with payload encoded in JSON format. Geth allows connectivity to JSON RPC using the following three different protocols:

- **Inter Process Communication (IPC)**: This protocol is used for inter process communication generally used within the same computer.
- **Remote Procedure Calls (RPC)**: This protocol is used for inter process communication across computers. This is generally based on TCP and HTTP protocol.
- **Web Sockets (WS)**: This protocol is used to connect to Geth using sockets.

There are many commands, switches, and options for configuring Geth, which include the following:

- Configuring IPC, RPC, and WS protocols
- Configuring network types to connect—private, Ropster, and Rinkeby
- Mining options
- Console and API
- Networking
- Debugging and logging

Some of the important options for creating a private network will be discussed in the next section.

Geth can be used to connect to a public network by just running `Geth` without any options. Homestead is the current name of public Ethereum. Its `networkid` and `ChainID` is 1 as shown in the following screenshot:

```
C:\Users\citynextadmin>Geth
WARN [11-13|07:53:00] No etherbase set and no accounts found as default
INFO [11-13|07:53:01] Starting peer-to-peer node              instance=Geth/v1.7.2-stable-1db4ecdc/windows-amd64/go1.9
INFO [11-13|07:53:01] Allocated cache and file handles        database=C:\\Users\\citynextadmin\\AppData\\Roaming\\Ethe
reum\\geth\\chaindata cache=128 handles=1024
INFO [11-13|07:53:01] Initialised chain configuration         config="{ChainID: 1 Homestead: 1150000 DAO: 1920000 DAOSu
pport: true EIP150: 2463000 EIP155: 2675000 EIP158: 2675000 Byzantium: 4370000 Engine: ethash}"
INFO [11-13|07:53:01] Disk storage enabled for ethash caches  dir=C:\\Users\\citynextadmin\\AppData\\Roaming\\Ethereum\
\geth\\ethash count=3
INFO [11-13|07:53:01] Disk storage enabled for ethash DAGs    dir=C:\\Users\\citynextadmin\\AppData\\Ethash
                 count=2
INFO [11-13|07:53:02] Initialising Ethereum protocol          versions="[63 62]" network=1
INFO [11-13|07:53:02] Loaded most recent local header         number=0 hash=d4e567...cb8fa3 td=17179869184
INFO [11-13|07:53:02] Loaded most recent local full block     number=0 hash=d4e567...cb8fa3 td=17179869184
INFO [11-13|07:53:02] Loaded most recent local fast block     number=0 hash=d4e567...cb8fa3 td=17179869184
INFO [11-13|07:53:02] Loaded local transaction journal        transactions=0 dropped=0
INFO [11-13|07:53:02] Regenerated local transaction journal   transactions=0 accounts=0
INFO [11-13|07:53:02] Starting P2P networking
```

The following are the network IDs used for connecting to the following different networks:

- The chain ID 1 represents a Homestead public network
- The chain ID 2 represents Morden (not used anymore)
- The chain ID 3 represents Ropsten
- The chain ID 4 represents Rinkeby
- The chain ID above 4 represents a private network

Geth provides the `--testnet` option to connect to a Ropsten network and the `--rinkeby` option to connect to the Rinkeby option. These should be used in conjunction with the `networkid` command option.

Creating a private network

After Geth is installed, it can be configured to run locally without connecting to any network on the internet. Every chain and network has a genesis block or the first block. This block does not have any parent and is the first block of the chain. A `genesis.json` file is required to create this first block. A sample `genesis.json` file is shown in the following code snippet:

```
{
"config": {
"chainId": 15,
"homesteadBlock": 0,
"eip155Block": 0,
"eip158Block": 0
},
"nonce": "0x0000000000000042",
"mixhash":
"0x0000000000000000000000000000000000000000000000000000000000000000",
"difficulty": "0x200",
"alloc": {},
"coinbase": "0x0000000000000000000000000000000000000000",
"timestamp": "0x00",
"parentHash":
"0x0000000000000000000000000000000000000000000000000000000000000000",
"gasLimit": "0xffffffff",
"alloc": {
}
}
```

Let's take a look at the following steps to create a private network:

1. The `genesis.json` file should be passed to Geth to initialize the private network. The Geth node also needs to store the blockchain data and account keys. This information should also be provided to Geth while initializing the private network.

2. The following `geth init` command initializes the node with the `genesis.json` file and target data directory location to store the chaindata and keystore information:

    ```
    C:\Windows\system32>geth init "C:\myeth\genesis.json" --datadir
    "C:\myeth\chaindata"
    ```

    The preceding command line will generate the following output:

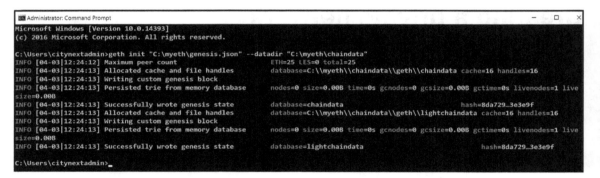

3. After the Geth node is initialized with the genesis block as shown in the preceding screenshot, Geth can be started. Geth uses IPC protocol by default and will be enabled. For ensuring that the Geth node is reachable using RPC protocol, RPC options need to be provided explicitly.

4. For setting up an environment as a Geth node, execute the following command line:

    ```
    geth --datadir "C:\myeth\chaindata" --rpc --rpcapi "eth,web3,miner,
    admin,personal,net" --rpccorsdomain "*" --nodiscover --networkid 15
    ```

The preceding command line will generate the following output:

```
Administrator: Command Prompt - geth --datadir "C:\myeth\chaindata" --rpc --rpcapi "eth,web3,miner,admin,personal,net" --rpccorsdomain "*" --nodiscover --n...    —    □    ×
omain "*" --nodiscover --networkid 15
INFO [04-03|12:28:05] Maximum peer count                       ETH=25 LES=0 total=25
INFO [04-03|12:28:05] Starting peer-to-peer node               instance=Geth/v1.8.1-stable-1e67410e/windows-amd64/go1.9.
2
INFO [04-03|12:28:05] Allocated cache and file handles         database=C:\\myeth\\chaindata\\geth\\chaindata cache=768
handles=1024
INFO [04-03|12:28:05] Initialised chain configuration          config="{ChainID: 15 Homestead: 0 DAO: <nil> DAOSupport:
false EIP150: <nil> EIP155: 0 EIP158: 0 Byzantium: <nil> Engine: unknown}"
INFO [04-03|12:28:05] Disk storage enabled for ethash caches   dir=C:\\myeth\\chaindata\\geth\\ethash count=3
INFO [04-03|12:28:05] Disk storage enabled for ethash DAGs     dir=C:\\Users\\citynextadmin\\AppData\\Ethash count=2
INFO [04-03|12:28:05] Initialising Ethereum protocol           versions="[63 62]" network=15
INFO [04-03|12:28:05] Loaded most recent local header          number=0 hash=8da729...3e3e9f td=512
INFO [04-03|12:28:05] Loaded most recent local full block      number=0 hash=8da729...3e3e9f td=512
INFO [04-03|12:28:05] Loaded most recent local fast block      number=0 hash=8da729...3e3e9f td=512
INFO [04-03|12:28:05] Loaded local transaction journal         transactions=0 dropped=0
INFO [04-03|12:28:05] Regenerated local transaction journal    transactions=0 accounts=0
INFO [04-03|12:28:05] Starting P2P networking
INFO [04-03|12:28:05] HTTP endpoint opened                     url=http://127.0.0.1:8545 cors=* vhosts=localhost
INFO [04-03|12:28:05] RLPx listener up                         self="enode://b229dac3769c7723b79614c36d07b3c7876a80cee0d
412eeb23dad8b3d2f76437334046ca9d73973814262724d7b846903ad249ff0f222ea32b49684cbaf8dc80[::]:30303?discport=0"
INFO [04-03|12:28:05] IPC endpoint opened                      url=\\\\.\\pipe\\geth.ipc
```

There are a lot of important activities happening when this command is executed. The command is executed with the `datadir` information, enabling RPC, modules, and APIs that are exposed from this node instance when using RPC to connect, and `networkid` of 15 denoting that it is a private network. The result of executing this command also provides useful insights. First, the etherbase or coinbase is not set. The coinbase or etherbase account should be created and set before mining is started. As of now, mining has not started although it was possible to auto-start mining with this command itself. The information about current database location is printed on the screen. The output also displays `ChainID` and whether it is connected to a Homestead public network. A value of zero means it is not connected to a Homestead network. The output also contains the enode value, which is a node identifier on the network. If more nodes want to join this network, they should provide this enode value to join this chain and network. Toward the end, the output shows that both IPC and RPC protocols are up and running and accepting requests. The RPC endpoint is available at `http://127.0.0.1:8545` or `http://localhost:8545` and IPC is available at `\\.\pipe\geth.ipc`. Take a look at the following command line:

```
geth --datadir "C:\myeth\chaindata" --rpc --rpcapi
"eth,web3,miner,admin,personal,net" --rpccorsdomain "*" --
nodiscover --networkid 15
```

5. The preceding command will get the private Ethereum node up and running. However, astute readers will notice that the command runs as a service. Additional commands cannot be executed through it. To manage existing running Geth nodes, open another command window on the same computer and type the `Geth attach ipc:\\.\pipe\geth.ipc` command for connecting using IPC protocol. You will get the following output:

```
Administrator: Command Prompt - geth attach ipc:\\.\pipe\geth.ipc

C:\Users\citynextadmin>geth attach
Fatal: Unable to attach to remote geth: no known transport for URL scheme "c"

C:\Users\citynextadmin>geth attach ipc:\\.\pipe\geth.ipc
Welcome to the Geth JavaScript console!

instance: Geth/v1.8.1-stable-1e67410e/windows-amd64/go1.9.2
 modules: admin:1.0 debug:1.0 eth:1.0 miner:1.0 net:1.0 personal:1.0 rpc:1.0 txpool:1.0 web3:1.0
```

6. To connect to a private Geth instance through RPC endpoint, use the command `Geth attach rpc:http://localhost:8545` or use `Geth attach rpc:http://127.0.0.1:8545` to connect to a local running instance of Ethereum. If you see a different output than shown here, it's because the coinbase account is already set in my case. Adding a coinbase account is shown later in this section.

7. The default RPC port on which these endpoints are hosted is `8545`, which can be changed using the `-rpcport` Geth command line option. The IP address can be changed using the `-rpcaddr` option:

```
Administrator: Command Prompt - geth attach rpc:http://127.0.0.1:8545

C:\Users\citynextadmin>geth attach rpc:http://127.0.0.1:8545
Welcome to the Geth JavaScript console!

instance: Geth/v1.7.2-stable-1db4ecdc/windows-amd64/go1.9
coinbase: 0x3d878119b2cda3b8cab055861713cd100efbe71c
at block: 148 (Sun, 12 Nov 2017 09:23:42 GMT)
 datadir: C:\myeth\chaindata
 modules: admin:1.0 eth:1.0 miner:1.0 net:1.0 personal:1.0 rpc:1.0 web3:1.0

>
```

8. After connecting to a Geth node, it's time to set up the coinbase or etherbase account. For this, a new account should be created first. To create a new account, use the `newAccount` method of the `personal` object. While creating a new account, provide `passphrase` that acts like a password for the account. The output of this execution is the account ID as shown in the following screenshot:

```
> personal.newAccount()
Passphrase:
Repeat passphrase:
"0xe14d4d757d493d300b11de058f7cba464c0effc8"
```

9. With the account ID provisioned, it should be tagged as a coinbase or etherbase account. To do this, the Geth provider has to change the coinbase `address.miner` object with the `setEtherBase` function. This method will change the current coinbase to the provided account. The output of the command is `true` or `false` as shown in the following screenshot:

```
> miner.setEtherbase("0xe14d4d757d493d300b11de058f7cba464c0effc8")
true
>
```

10. Now run the following query to find the current `coinbase` account by executing the following command:

```
eth.coinbase
```

It should output the same account address that was recently created as shown in the following screenshot:

```
> eth.coinbase
"0xe14d4d757d493d300b11de058f7cba464c0effc8"
>
```

With the coinbase set with a valid account and Geth node up and running, now mining can get started and, since we just have one miner, all rewards will go to this miner and its coinbase account will be credited with Ethers.

11. To start mining, execute the following command:

```
miner.start()
```

You can also use the following command line:

```
miner.start(4)
```

The preceding command line generates the following output:

```
> miner.start(4)
null
>
```

The parameter to the `start` method represents the number of threads used for mining. This will result in mining getting started and the same can be viewed from the original command window:

```
INFO [11-13|12:38:31] RLPx listener up                          self=enode://87d6158dc33c3d308bde58c8a107a883a0
fcccc754cbc33513e097d58cebb77bf571e76ff4101793ccecffd8edcd8f40947dfce7d8f52485140bb449f9@[::]:30303
INFO [11-13|12:38:32] IPC endpoint opened: \\.\pipe\geth.ipc
INFO [11-13|12:52:18] Updated mining threads                    threads=4
INFO [11-13|12:52:18] Transaction pool price threshold updated  price=18000000000
INFO [11-13|12:52:18] Starting mining operation
INFO [11-13|12:52:18] Commit new mining work                    number=149 txs=0 uncles=0 elapsed=0s
```

12. Mining can be stopped from the second command window using the `miner.stop()` command.

ganache-cli

There are following two distinct phases in the overall modification and writing of transactions to a ledger using Ethereum:

- The first stage is about creating a transaction and putting the transaction in a transaction pool.
- The second phase that happens periodically is to get all transactions from a transaction pool and mine them. Mining here means writing those transactions to the Ethereum database or ledger.

From this description, it would be a time-consuming process if the same process is used for development and testing purposes. To ease the process of development and test of solutions and smart contracts on Ethereum, ganache-cli was created. It was earlier known as TestRPC. ganache-cli by itself contains both the Ethereum transaction processing and mining functionality. Moreover, there is no waiting period for mining of transactions. The transactions are written as they are generated. It means developers can use ganache-cli as their Ethereum node and do not need mining activity to write transactions to a ledger. Instead, the transactions are stored in a ledger as they are created.

ganache-cli is dependent on Node.js and it should be available on the machine before deploying ganache-cli. If Node.js is not installed, it can be downloaded from `https://nodejs.org/en/download/`. Based on processor architecture (32 or 64 bit) and operating system, an appropriate package can be downloaded and installed from the given link as shown in the following screenshot:

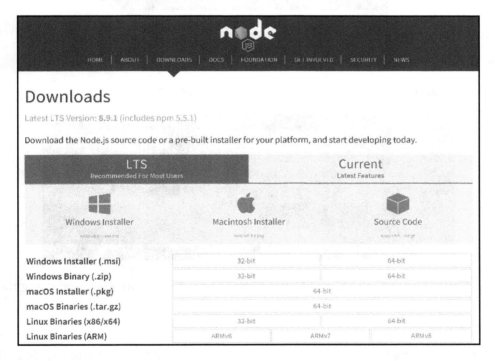

Here, we have downloaded the 64 bit version of MSI Windows installer and both **node package manager** (**NPM**) and Node.js are installed using it.

The Node.js version is `v8.9.1` as shown in the following screenshot:

```
C:\Users\citynextadmin>node --version
v8.9.1

C:\Users\citynextadmin>
```

The npm version is `5.5.1` as shown in the following screenshot:

```
C:\Users\citynextadmin>npm --version
5.5.1

C:\Users\citynextadmin>
```

ganache-cli can be installed using the following `npm install` command:

```
npm install -g ganache-cli
```

The preceding command line generates the following output:

```
C:\Users\citynextadmin>npm install -g ganache-cli
npm WARN deprecated babel-preset-es2015@6.24.1: 
npm WARN deprecated nomnom@1.8.1: Package no longer
C:\Users\citynextadmin\AppData\Roaming\npm\ganache-
npm WARN webpack-cli@2.0.13 requires a peer of webp

+ ganache-cli@6.1.0
added 492 packages in 70.513s
```

After installation of ganache-cli, an Ethereum node based on it can be started using the following command:

```
ganache-cli
```

The result of executing the preceding command is that it creates 10 accounts by default, each having 100 Ether in balance with them, and it can be used just the way any other private network is used as shown in the following screenshot:

```
C:\Users\citynextadmin>ganache-cli
Ganache CLI v6.1.0 (ganache-core: 2.1.0)

Available Accounts
==================
(0) 0xb2d4fc1bd4971715d4bf67662926b603060fa7e5
(1) 0x400e4d8a1affcec6495bdab627092c139f9c5897
(2) 0x9502159df7cf412132c0b79200ea478b2357dc37
(3) 0xb260a5fe0be2c32667553f836cdc0b52d74befa0
(4) 0x5954c37e2c5dacc2e5a67dc548fd9a393ae70cb7
(5) 0x9f9064d0e6fb2b157db28b6d0424f5087b834ff1
(6) 0xfc8279e0a9976bd51516310b64f23e7459a8cd00
(7) 0xcb4ad724e7e38c1d31770d64578fa50658153219
(8) 0xcce2e065b44d865cbff56a746680bf883f37027a
(9) 0x8fa1b27a7458a5f5cc707763d95cba6d7cfd87d4

Private Keys
==================
(0) 2694d75fa257a63a2e6da1e14ff9b85dcacb7885a659b10e92902541ad433769
(1) e99109f2e419d9243ab319563946b19debfbf39b7808748c65a120a9216597e4
(2) bd448b10725f555f14fbce0b43ce6e04bdd8386926eabb6d1682855b23d52ede
(3) 7c7f645f2aedc3fd89226af07f3b6ae599badf5a74021b377b250f1ad8e3e6a0
(4) 02cc9f83052130e00a95d5f02c6053b9f6c7bc2d40bcb0c454c8cf7f9f48d81c
(5) a8a2984b371d5deb4db984e3ac7dcee7a2ab730a2025aef0cf9ea475c74ec1e7
(6) eadc6697222450bc2cfeeceb999e6ad909fd9916f801ef567c67677fcf0b41d2
(7) f8e486cdff58764bd28d73a855473c29cabf3316076777ef54e858428e64295e
(8) 481186bd532f8d3c9149dbbe8e3afd4daf74034a3d368a17606b38fc6c4e7686
(9) fe5fc2dd37407169bf512622a7ba66a1b70ab54c9c3b6ba56e410c10304dcb6a
```

Another command window can be used along with the Geth command line to attach to it, just like in the following screenshot:

```
Administrator: Command Prompt - geth  attach rpc:http://127.0.0.1:8545

C:\Users\citynextadmin>geth attach rpc:http://127.0.0.1:8545
Welcome to the Geth JavaScript console!

instance: Geth/v1.7.2-stable-1db4ecdc/windows-amd64/go1.9
coinbase: 0x3d878119b2cda3b8cab055861713cd100efbe71c
at block: 148 (Sun, 12 Nov 2017 09:23:42 GMT)
 datadir: C:\myeth\chaindata
 modules: admin:1.0 eth:1.0 miner:1.0 net:1.0 personal:1.0 rpc:1.0 web3:1.0

>
```

Solidity compiler

Solidity is one of the languages that is used to author smart contracts. Smart contracts will be dealt with in detail in the following chapters. The code written using Solidity is compiled using a Solidity compiler, which outputs byte code and other artifacts needed for deployment of smart contracts. Earlier, Solidity was part of the Geth installation; however, it has moved out of Geth and should be deployed using its own installation.

The Solidity compiler also known as `solc` can be installed using `npm`:

```
npm install -g solc
```

The preceding command line generates the following output:

```
C:\Users\citynextadmin>npm install -g solc
C:\Users\citynextadmin\AppData\Roaming\npm\solcjs -> C:\Users\citynextadmin\AppData\Roaming\npm\node_modules\solc\solcjs
+ solc@0.4.18
added 65 packages in 17.147s

C:\Users\citynextadmin>_
```

The web3 JavaScript library

The `web3` library is an open source JavaScript library that can be used to connect to Ethereum nodes from the same or a remote computer. It allows IPC as well as RPC to connect to Ethereum nodes. `web3` is a client-side library and can be used alongside a web page and query and can submit transactions to Ethereum nodes. It can be installed using the node package manager as a node module like the Solidity compiler. At the time of writing, the latest version of `web3` is broken and does not install appropriately because of the missing `BigNumber.js` file. However, previous stable versions can be used for connecting web applications to backend Ethereum nodes. Let's take a look at the following steps to install the `web3` JavaScript library:

1. The command used to install `web3` is as follows:

```
npm install web3@0.19
```

The preceding command generates the following output:

```
C:\Users\citynextadmin>npm install web3@0.19
npm WARN saveError ENOENT: no such file or directory, open 'C:\Users\citynextadmin\package.json'
npm WARN enoent ENOENT: no such file or directory, open 'C:\Users\citynextadmin\package.json'
npm WARN citynextadmin No description
npm WARN citynextadmin No repository field.
npm WARN citynextadmin No README data
npm WARN citynextadmin No license field.

+ web3@0.19.1
updated 1 package in 2.681s

C:\Users\citynextadmin>
```

2. After `web3` is installed, it can be used using Node.js. From Command Prompt, enter the node workspace by executing the `node` command as shown in the following screenshot:

```
C:\Users\citynextadmin>node
>
```

3. Once in the node workspace, type the following commands to connect to an Ethereum node. The Ethereum node could be TestRPC or a custom Geth-based private network. `web3` can use WebSockets, IPC, or RPC to connect to an Ethereum node. The following example shows the RPC endpoint protocol used to connect `web3` to an Ethereum node:

```
var Web = require('web3')
var web = new Web (new
Web.providers.HttpProvider('http://localhost:8545'))
```

The first command loads the `web3` module and the second command creates an instance of `HttpProvider` and connects to the local hosted Ethereum node on port `8545`.

4. To ensure that `web3` is actually connected to an Ethereum node, execute the `isConnected` method. If it returns `true` then it means that `web3` is connected as shown in the following screenshot:

```
Administrator: Command Prompt - node
Microsoft Windows [Version 10.0.14393]
(c) 2016 Microsoft Corporation. All rights reserved.

C:\Users\citynextadmin>node
> var Web = require('web3')
undefined
> var web = new Web (new Web.providers.HttpProvider('http://localhost:8545'))
undefined
> web.isConnected()
true
>
```

Mist wallet

Ethereum works with Ether cryptocurrency and a wallet is required to send and receive Ether. Mist is an implementation of the same. Mist is a wallet used to send and receive Ether. It helps in executing transactions on the Ethereum network. The network can be public or private. It allows users to create their accounts, send and receive Ether, and deploy and invoke contracts.

Mist can be downloaded from `https://github.com/ethereum/mist/releases`. Download an appropriate ZIP file (in this case it is `Ethereum-Wallet-win64-0-9-2.zip` since we are deploying on Windows 2016) and extract to a file location. Double-click on the **Ethereum Wallet** application from the extracted files as shown in the following screenshot:

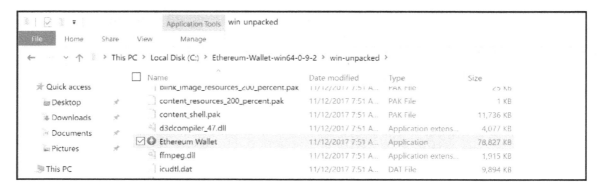

This should start Mist. Mist is an intelligent wallet. If a private chain is running on a local machine then it can identify the same and connect to it. If there is no local network running, then it will connect to the main network or Rinkeby test network:

However, if a private network is available, it will connect to it as shown in the following screenshot:

Once connected, it can be used to interact with an Ethereum network by sending and receiving Ether, and deploying and invoking functions of smart contracts:

MetaMask

MetaMask is a lightweight Chrome browser-based extension that helps in interacting with Ethereum networks. It is also a wallet that helps in sending and receiving Ether. MetaMask can be downloaded from `https://metamask.io/`. Since MetaMask runs in a browser, it does not download the entire chaindata locally; instead, it stores it centrally and helps users connect to their store using the browser. Let's take a look at the following steps:

1. MetaMask should be added as an extension as shown in the following screenshot:

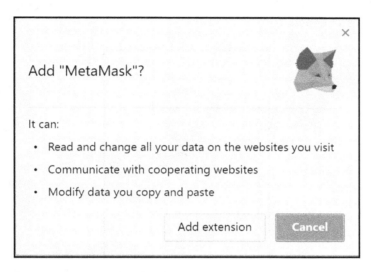

2. Accept the privacy notice and terms of use and a small icon will appear next to the go button. MetaMask allows you to connect to multiple networks. Connect to the **Localhost 8545** private network as shown in the following screenshot:

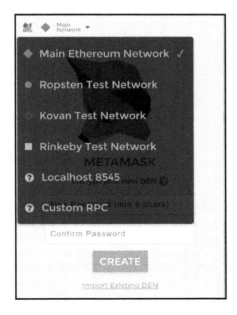

3. Provide a password to create a new key that is used by MetaMask to identify the user. It is stored in a key vault at the MetaMask central server as shown in the following screenshot:

4. Click on the **Account** icon and import all already created accounts using the **Import Account** menu in MetaMask:

5. After all the accounts are created, MetaMask can be used to transfer Ether from one account to another using Ethereum transactions.

6. For sending Ether from one account to another, select an account and click on the **Send** button. On the resultant window, provide a target account address, amount, and click on the **Next** button:

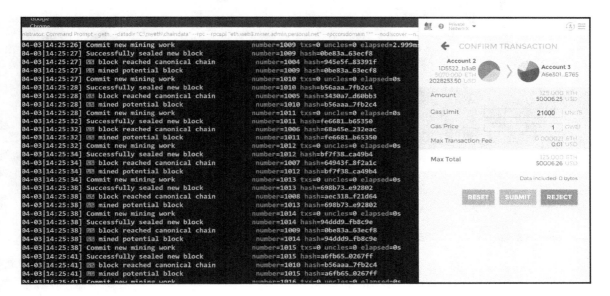

7. Submit the transaction. The transaction will be in a pending state within the transaction pool. Mining should be started to write this transaction into the permanent storage.

8. Start mining using the Geth console and the transaction will be mined as shown in the following screenshot:

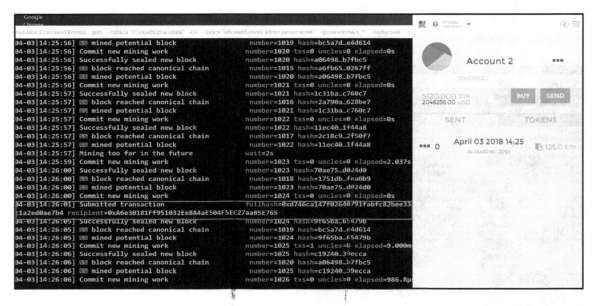

After a while the transaction is written in the ledger, and balances for both the accounts are updated in MetaMask:

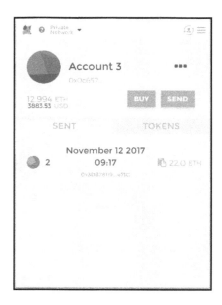

Summary

There was a lot of substance covered in this chapter. Ethereum nodes implement JSON RPC endpoints that can be connected to using WebSockets, IPC, and RPC. In this chapter, we discussed various forms of networks—public, main, test, and private. The chapter also discusses and implements a private network. This chapter had steps to create a development environment that will be used later in subsequent chapters. This chapter focuses on deploying multiple tools and utilities on the Windows operating system. While each tool has its own working and functionality, some tools might eventually do the same thing. For example, a Geth-based private chain and ganache-cli are essentially Ethereum nodes but with differences. Deployment of Geth, Solidity compiler, ganache-cli, `web3` JavaScript framework, Mist, and MetaMask were covered in this chapter. While some readers will like working with ganache-cli, others will be interested in using a private Geth-based Ethereum node. There is another important utility known as Truffle that will be covered in subsequent chapters.

In the next chapter, we will focus on Solidity as a language, which is the title of the book. Solidity supports object orientation, provides both native as well as complex data types, helps in declaring and defining functions that accept parameters and return values, provides control structures and expressions, and many more features. The next chapter will discuss variables and data types in depth. The variables and data types are core to any programming language and more so in Solidity since it has to store the same within the distributed ledger.

Introducing Solidity
3

From this chapter, we will embark on a journey: learning the Solidity language. The previous two chapters introduced blockchains, Ethereum, and their toolsets. Some important concepts related to blockchains, which are essential for having a better understanding and writing efficient code in Solidity, were also discussed. There are multiple languages that target EVM. Some of them are deprecated and others are used with varying degrees of acceptance. Solidity is by far the most popular language for EVM. From this chapter onward, the book will focus on Solidity and its concepts, as well as constructs to help write efficient smart contracts.

In this chapter, we will jump right into understanding Solidity, its structure, data types, and variables. We will cover the following topics in this chapter:

- Solidity and Solidity files
- Structure of a contract
- Data types in Solidity
- Storage and memory data locations
- Literals
- Integers
- Boolean
- The byte data type
- Arrays
- Structure of an array
- Enumeration
- Address
- Mappings

Ethereum Virtual Machine

Solidity is a programming language targeting Ethereum Virtual Machine (EVM). Ethereum blockchain helps extend its functionality by writing and executing code known as smart contracts. We will get into the details of smart contracts in subsequent chapters, but for now, it is enough to know that smart contracts are similar to object-oriented classes written in Java or C++.

EVM executes code that is part of smart contracts. Smart contracts are written in Solidity; however, EVM does not understand the high-level constructs of Solidity. EVM understands lower-level instructions called **bytecode**.

Solidity code needs a compiler to take its code and convert it into bytecode that is understandable by EVM. Solidity comes with a compiler to do this job, known as the Solidity compiler or solc. We downloaded and installed the Solidity compiler in the last chapter using the Node.js npm command.

The entire process is shown in the following diagram, from writing code in Solidity to executing it in EVM:

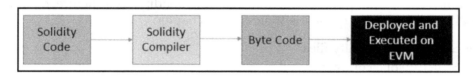

We have already explored our first Solidity code in the last chapter, when writing our HelloWorld contract.

Solidity and Solidity files

Solidity is a programming language that is very close to JavaScript. Similarities between JavaScript and C can be found within Solidity. Solidity is a statically-typed, case-sensitive, and **object-oriented programming (OOP)** language. Although it is object-oriented, it supports limited objected orientation features. What this means is that variable data types should be defined and known at compile time. Functions and variables should be written in OOP same way as they are defined. In Solidity, Cat is different from CAT, cat, or any other variation of cat. The statement terminator in Solidity is the semicolon: ; .

Solidity code is written in Solidity files that have the extension .sol. They are human-readable text files that can be opened as text files in any editor including Notepad.

A Solidity file is composed of the following four high-level constructs:

- Pragma
- Comments
- Import
- Contracts/library/interface

Pragma

Pragma is generally the first line of code within any Solidity file. pragma is a directive that specifies the compiler version to be used for current Solidity file.

Solidity is a new language and is subject to continuous improvement on an on-going basis. Whenever a new feature or improvement is introduced, it comes out with a new version. The current version at the time of writing was 0.4.19.

With the help of the `pragma` directive, you can choose the compiler version and target your code accordingly, as shown in the following code example:

```
pragma Solidity ^0.4.19;
```

Although it is not mandatory, it is a good practice to declare the `pragma` directive as the first statement in a Solidity file.

The syntax for the `pragma` directive is as follows:

```
pragma Solidity <<version number>> ;
```

Also notice the case-sensitivity of the directive. Both `pragma` and `Solidity` are in small letters, with a valid version number and statement terminated with a semicolon.

The version number comprises of two numbers—a **major build** and a **minor build** number.

The major build number in the preceding example is 4 and the minor build number is 19. Generally, there are fewer or no breaking changes within minor versions but there could be significant changes between major versions. You should choose a version that best suits your requirements.

The ^ character, also known as **caret**, is optional in version numbers but plays a significant role in deciding the version number based on the following rules:

- The ^ character refers to the latest version within a major version. So, ^0.4.0 refers to the latest version within build number 4, which currently would be 0.4.19.
- The ^ character will not target any other major build apart from the one that is provided.
- The Solidity file will compile only with a compiler with 4 as the major build. It will not compile with any other major build.

As a good practice, it is better to compile Solidity code with an exact compiler version rather than using ^. There are changes in newer version that could deprecate your code while using ^ in `pragma`. For example, the `throw` statement got deprecated and newer constructs such as `assert`, `require`, and `revert` were recommended for use in newer versions. You do not want to get surprised on a day when your code starts behaving differently.

Comments

Any programming language provides the facility to comment code and so does Solidity. There are the following three types of comment in Solidity:

- Single-line comments
- Multiline comments
- **Ethereum Natural Specification (Natspec)**

Single-line comments are denoted by a double forward slash //, while multiline comments are denoted using /* and */. Natspec has two formats: /// for single-line and a combination of /** for beginning and */ for end of multiline comments. Natspec is used for documentation purposes and it has its own specification. The entire specification is available at `https://github.com/ethereum/wiki/wiki/Ethereum-Natural-Specification-Format`.

Let's take a look at Solidity comments in the following code:

```
// This is a single-line comment in Solidity
/* This is a multiline comment
In Solidity. Use this when multiple consecutive lines
Should be commented as a whole */
```

In Remix, the `pragma` directive and comments are as shown in the following screenshot:

```
« ± browser/PragmaAndComments.sol ✕

1
2
3
4    pragma solidity 0.4.19;
5
6    // This is a single line comment in Solidity
7
8 ▾  /* This is a multi-line comment
9       In solidity. Use this when multiple consecutive lines
10   Should be commented as a whole */
11
12
13   |
```

The import statement

The `import` keyword helps import other Solidity files and we can access its code within the current Solidity file and code. This helps us write modular Solidity code.

The syntax for using `import` is as follows:

```
import <<filename>> ;
```

File names can be fully explicit or implicit paths. The forward slash / is used for separating directories from other directories and files while . is used to refer to the current directory and .. is used to refer to the parent directory. This is very similar to the Linux bash way of referring to a file. A typical `import` statement is shown here. Also, note the semicolon towards the end of the statement in the following code:

```
import 'CommonLibrary.sol';
```

Contracts

Apart from `pragma`, `import`, and comments, we can define contracts, libraries, and interfaces at the global or top level. We will explore contracts, libraries, and interfaces in depth in subsequent chapters. This chapter assumes that you understand that multiple contracts, libraries, and interfaces can be declared within the same Solidity file. The `library`, `contract`, and `interface` keywords shown in the following screenshot are case-sensitive in nature:

```
//contracts.sol

pragma solidity 0.4.19;

// This is a single line comment in Solidity

/* This is a multi-line comment
    In solidity. Use this when multiple consecutive lines
Should be commented as a whole */

contract firstContract {

}

contract secondContract {

}

library stringLibrary {

}

library mathLibrary {

}

interface IBank{

}

interface IAccount {

}
```

Structure of a contract

The primary purpose of Solidity is to write smart contracts for Ethereum. Smart contracts are the basic unit of deployment and execution for EVMs. Although multiple chapters later in this book are dedicated to writing and developing smart contracts, the basic structure of smart contracts is discussed in this chapter.

Technically, smart contracts are composed of two constructs—variables and functions. There are multiple facets to both variables and functions and that is again something that will be discussed throughout this book. This section is about describing the general structure of a smart contract using the Solidity language.

A contract consists of the following multiple constructs:

- State variables
- Structure definitions
- Modifier definitions
- Event declarations
- Enumeration definitions
- Function definitions

A typical contract consists of all the preceding constructs. In the following screenshot, it is to be noted that each of these constructs in turn consists of multiple other constructs, which will be discussed in subsequent chapter when these topics are discussed in detail:

```solidity
pragma solidity 0.4.19;

//contract definition
contract generalStructure {
    //state variables
    int public stateIntVariable; // vriable of integer type
    string stateStringVariable; //variable of string type
    address personIdentifier; // variable of address type
    myStruct human; // variable of structure type
    bool constant hasIncome = true; //variable of constant nature

    //structure definition
    struct myStruct {
        string name; //variable fo type string
        uint myAge; // variable of unsigned integer type
        bool isMarried; // variable of boolean type
        uint[] bankAccountsNumbers; // variable - dynamic array of unsigned integer
    }

    //modifier declaration
    modifier onlyBy(){
        if (msg.sender == personIdentifier) {
            _;
        }
    }

    // event declaration
    event ageRead(address, int );

    //enumeration declaration
    enum gender {male, female}

    //function definition
    function getAge (address _personIdentifier) onlyBy() payable external returns (uint) {

        human = myStruct("Ritesh",10,true,new uint[](3)); //using struct myStruct

        gender _gender = gender.male; //using enum

        ageRead(personIdentifier, stateIntVariable);
    }
}
```

State variables

Variables in programming refer to storage location that can contain values. These values can be changed during runtime. The variable can be used at multiple places within code and they will all refer to the value stored within it. Solidity provides two types of variable—state and memory variables. In this section, we will introduce state variables.

One of the most important aspects of Solidity contracts is state variables. It is these state variables that are permanently stored in a blockchain/Ethereum ledger by miners. Variables declared in a contract that are not within any function are called **state variables**. State variables store the current values of the contract. The allocated memory for a state variable is statically assigned and it cannot change (the size of memory allocated) during the lifetime of the contract. Each state variable has a type that must be defined statically. The Solidity compiler must ascertain the memory allocation details for each state variables and so the state variable data type must be declared.

State variables also have additional qualifiers associated with them. They can be any one of the following:

- `internal`: By default, the state variable has the `internal` qualifier if nothing is specified. It means that this variable can only be used within current contract functions and any contract that inherits from them. These variables cannot be accessed from outside for modification; however, they can be viewed. An example of internal state variable is as follows:

    ```
    int internal StateVariable ;
    ```

- `private`: This qualifier is like `internal` with additional constraints. Private state variables can only be used in contracts declaring them. They cannot be used even within derived contracts. An example of a private state variable is as follows:

    ```
    int private privateStateVariable ;
    ```

- `public`: This qualifier makes state variables access directly. The Solidity compiler generates a `getter` function for each public state variable. An example of a public state variable is as follows:

    ```
    int public stateIntVariable ;
    ```

- `constant`: This qualifier makes state variables immutable. The value must be assigned to the variable at declaration time itself. In fact, the compiler will replace references of this variable everywhere in code with the assigned value. An example of a constant state variable is as follows:

```
bool constant hasIncome = true;
```

As mentioned previously, each state variable has an associated data type. A data type helps us determine the memory requirements for the variable and ascertain the values that can be stored in them. For example, a state variable of type `uint8` also known as **unsigned integer** is allocated a predetermined memory size and it can contain values ranging from 0 to 255. Any other value is regarded as foreign and is not acceptable by compiler and runtime for storing it in this variable.

Solidity provides the following multiple out-of-box data types:

- `bool`
- `uint/int`
- `bytes`
- `address`
- `mapping`
- `enum`
- `struct`
- `bytes/String`

Using `enum` and `struct`, it is possible to declare custom user-defined data types as well. Later in this chapter, a complete section has been dedicated to data types and variables.

Structure

Structures or structs helps implement custom user-defined data types. A structure is a composite data type, consisting of multiple variables of different data types. They are very similar to contracts; however, they do not contain any code within them. They consist of only variables.

There are times when you would like to store related data together. Suppose you want to store information about an employee, say the employee name, age, marriage status, and bank account numbers. To represent this, these individual variables related to single employee, a structure in Solidity can be declared using the `struct` keyword. The variables within a structure are defined within opening and closing { } brackets as shown in the following screenshot:

```
//structure definition
struct myStruct {
    string name; //variable fo type string
    uint myAge; // variable of unsigned integer type
    bool isMarried; // variable of boolean type
    uint[] bankAccountsNumbers; // variable - dynamic array of unsigned integer
}
```

To create an instance of a structure, the following syntax is used. There is no need to explicitly use the `new` keyword. The `new` keyword can only be used to create an instance of contracts or arrays as shown in the following screenshot:

```
human = myStruct("Ritesh",10,true,new uint[](3)); //using struct myStruct
```

Multiple instance of `struct` can be created in functions. Structs can contain array and the `mapping` variables, while mappings and arrays can store values of type `struct`.

Modifiers

In Solidity, a modifier is always associated with a function. A modifier in programming languages refers to a construct that changes the behavior of the executing code. Since a modifier is associated with a function in Solidity, it has the power to change the behavior of functions that it is associated with. For easy understanding of modifiers, think of them as a function that will be executed before execution of the target function. Suppose you want to invoke the `getAge` function but, before executing it, you would like to execute another function that could check the current state of the contract, values in incoming parameters, the current value in state variables, and so on and accordingly decide whether the target function `getAge` should be executed. This helps in writing cleaner functions without cluttering them with validation and verification rules. Moreover, the modifier can be associated with multiple functions. This ensures cleaner, more readable, and more maintainable code.

A modifier is defined using the `modifier` keyword followed by the `modifier` identifier, any parameters it should accept, and then code within the `{}` brackets. An _ underscore in a modifier means: execute the target function. You can think of this as the underscore being replaced by the target function inline. `payable` is an out-of-the-box modifier provided by Solidity which when applied to any function allows that function to accept Ether.

A `modifier` keyword is declared at the contract level, as shown in the following screenshot:

```
//modifier declaration
modifier onlyBy(){
        if (msg.sender == personIdentifier) {
            _;
        }
}
```

As we can see, in the preceding screenshot of the code snippet, a modifier named `onlyBy()` is declared at the contract level. It checks the value of the incoming address using `msg.sender` with an address stored in the state variable. Some things such as `msg.sender` might not be understandable to readers; we will cover these in depth in the next chapter.

The modifier is associated with a `getAge` function as shown in the following screenshot:

```
//function definition
function getAge (address _personIdentifier) onlyBy() payable external returns (uint) {

    human = myStruct("Ritesh",10,true,new uint[](3)); //using struct myStruct

    gender _gender = gender.male; //using enum
}
```

The `getAge` function can only be executed by an account that has the same address as that stored in the contract's `_personIdentifier` state variable. The function will not be executed if any other account tries to invoke it.

It is to be noted that anybody can invoke the `getAge` function, but execution will only happen for single a account.

Events

Solidity supports events. Events in Solidity are just like events in other programming languages. Events are fired from contracts such that anybody interested in them can trap/catch them and execute code in response. Events in Solidity are used primarily for informing the calling application about the current state of the contract by means of the logging facility of EVM. They are used to notify applications about changes in contracts and applications can use them to execute their dependent logic. Instead of applications they keep polling the contract for certain state changes; the contract can inform them by means of events.

Events are declared within the contract at the global level and invoked within its functions. An event is declared using the `event` keyword, followed by an identifier and parameter list and terminated with a semicolon. The values in parameters can be used to log information or execute conditional logic. Event information and its values are stored as part of transactions within blocks. In the last chapter, while discussing the properties of a transaction, a property named `LogsBloom` was introduced. Events raised as part of a transaction are stored within this property.

There is no need to explicitly provide parameter variables—only data types are sufficient as shown in the following screenshot:

```
// event declaration
event ageRead(address, int );
```

An event can be invoked from any function by its name and by passing the required parameters, as shown in the following screenshot:

```
//function definition
function getAge (address _personIdentifier) onlyBy() payable external returns (uint) {

    human = myStruct("Ritesh",10,true,new uint[](3)); //using struct myStruct

    gender _gender = gender.male; //using enum

    ageRead(personIdentifier, stateIntVariable);
}
```

Enumeration

The `enum` keyword is used to declare enumerations. Enumerations help in declaring a custom user-defined data type in Solidity. `enum` consists of an enumeration list, a predetermined set of named constants.

Constant values within an `enum` can be explicitly converted into integers in Solidity. Each constant value gets an integer value, with the first one having a value of 0 and the value of each successive item is increased by 1.

An `enum` declaration uses the `enum` keyword followed by enumeration identifier and a list of enumeration values within the `{ }` brackets. It is to be noted that an `enum` declaration does not have a semicolon as its terminator and that there should be at least one member declared in the list.

An example of `enum` is as follows:

```
enum gender {male, female}
```

A variable of enumeration can be declared and assigned a value as shown in the following code:

```
gender _gender = gender.male ;
```

It is not mandatory to define `enum` in a Solidity contract. `enum` should be defined if there is a constant list of items that do not change like the example shown previously. These become good example for an `enum` declaration. They help make your code more readable and maintainable.

Functions

Functions are the heart of Ethereum and Solidity. Ethereum maintains the current state of state variables and executes transaction to change values in state variables. When a function in a contract is called or invoked, it results in the creation of a transaction. Functions are the mechanism to read and write values from/to state variables. Functions are a unit of code that can be executed on-demand by calling it. Functions can accept parameters, execute its logic, and optionally return values to the caller. They can be named as well as anonymous. Solidity provides named functions with the possibility of only one unnamed function in a contract called the fallback function. We will know more about fallback functions later in the book.

The syntax for declaring functions in Solidity is as follows:

```
//function definition
function getAge (address _personIdentifier) onlyBy() payable external returns (uint) {

}
```

A function is declared using the `function` keyword followed by its identifier—`getAge`, in this case. It can accept multiple comma-separated parameters. The parameter identifiers are optional, but data types should be provided in the parameter list. Functions can have modifiers attached, such as `onlyBy()` in this case.

There are a couple of additional qualifiers that affect the behavior and execution of a function. Functions have visibility qualifiers and qualifiers, related to what actions can be executed within the function. Both visibility and function ability-related keywords are discussed next. Functions can also return data and this information is declared using the `return` keyword, followed by list of return parameters. Solidity can return multiple parameters.

Functions has visibility qualifier associated with them similar to state variables. The visibility of a function can be any one of the following:

- `public`: This visibility makes function access directly from outside. They become part of the contracts interface and can be called both internally and externally.
- `internal`: By default, the state variable has `internal` qualifier if nothing is specified. It means that this function can only be used within the current contract and any contract that inherits from it. These functions cannot be accessed from outside. They are not part of the contracts interface.
- `private`: Private functions can only be used in contracts declaring them. They cannot be used even within derived contracts. They are not part of the contracts interface.
- `external`: This visibility makes function access directly from externally but not internally. These functions become part of the contracts interface.

Functions can also have the following additional qualifiers that change their behavior in terms of having the ability to change contract state variables:

- `constant`: These functions do not have the ability to modify the state of blockchain. They can read the state variables and return back to the caller, but they cannot modify any variable, invoke an event, create another contract, call other functions that can change state, and so on. Think of `constant` functions as functions that can read and return current state variable values.
- `view`: These functions are aliases of constant functions.
- `pure`: Pure functions further constraints the ability of functions. Pure functions can neither read and write—in short, they cannot access state variables. Functions that are declared with this qualifier should ensure that they will not access the current state and transaction variables.
- `payable`: Functions declared with the `payable` keyword has ability to accept Ether from the caller. The call will fail in case Ether is not provided by sender. A function can only accept Ether if it is marked as `payable`.

We will discuss the preceding qualifiers in detail in subsequent chapters.

Functions can be invoked by their names.

Data types in Solidity

Solidity data types can broadly be classified in the following two types:

- Value types
- Reference types

These two types in Solidity differ based on the way they are assigned to a variable and stored in EVM. Assigning a variable to another variable can be done by creating a new copy or just by coping the reference. Value types maintains independent copies of variables and changing the value in one variable does not effect value in another variable. However, changing values in reference type variables ensures that anybody referring to that variables gets updates value.

Value types

A type is referred as value type if it holds the data (value) directly within the memory owned by it. These types have values stored with them, instead of elsewhere. The same is illustrated in following diagram. In this example, a variable of data type **unsigned integer (uint)** is declared with **13** as its data(value). The variable **a** has memory space allocated by EVM which is referred as **0x123** and this location has the value **13** stored. Accessing this variable will provide us with the value **13** directly:

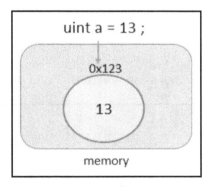

Value types are types that do not take more than 32 bytes of memory in size. Solidity provides the following value types:

- `bool`: The boolean value that can hold true or false as its value
- `uint`: These are unsigned integers that can hold 0 and positive values only
- `int`: These are signed integers that can hold both negative and positive values
- `address`: This represents an address of an account on Ethereum environment
- `byte`: This represents fixed sized byte array (`byte1` to `bytes32`)
- `enum`: Enumerations that can hold predefined constant values

Passing by value

When a value type variable is assigned to another variable or when a value type variable is sent as an argument to a function, EVM creates a new variable instance and copies the value of original value type into target variable. This is known as passing by value. Changing values in original or target variables will not affect the value in another variable. Both the variables will maintain their independent, isolated values and they can change without the other knowing about it.

Reference types

Reference types, unlike value types, do not store their values directly within the variabless themselves. Instead of the value, they store the address of the location where the value is stored. The variable holds the pointer to another memory location that holds the actual data. Reference types are types that can take more than 32 bytes of memory in size. Reference types are shown next, by means of an illustration.

In the following example, an array variable of data type **uint** is declared with size **6**. Arrays in Solidity are based at zero and so this array can hold seven elements. The variable **a** has memory space allocated by EVM which is referred as **0x123** and this location has a pointer value **0x456** stored in it. This pointer refers to the actual memory location where the array data is stored. When accessing the variable, EVM dereferences the value of the pointer and shows the value from the array index as shown in the following diagram:

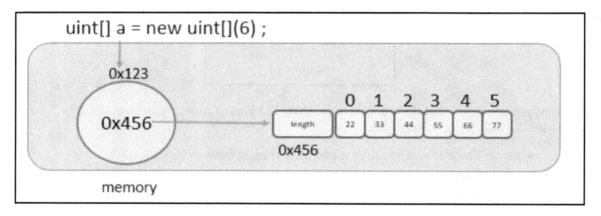

Solidity provides the following reference types:

- **Arrays**: These are fixed as well as dynamic arrays. Details are given later in this chapter.
- **Structs**: These are custom, user-defined structures.
- **String**: This is sequence of characters. In Solidity, strings are eventually stored as bytes. Details are give later in this chapter.
- **Mappings**: This is similar to a hash table or dictionary in other languages storing key-value pairs.

Passing by reference

When a reference type variable is assigned to another variable or when a reference type variable is sent as an argument to a function, EVM creates a new variable instance and copies the pointer from the original variable into the target variable. This is known as passing by reference. Both the variables are pointing to the same address location. Changing values in the original or target variables will change the value in other variables also. Both the variables will share the same values and change committed by one is reflected in the other variable.

Storage and memory data locations

Each variable declared and used within a contract has a data location. EVM provides the following four data structures for storing variables:

- **Storage**: This is global memory available to all functions within the contract. This storage is a permanent storage that Ethereum stores on every node within its environment.
- **Memory**: This is local memory available to every function within a contract. This is short lived and fleeting memory that gets torn down when the function completes its execution.
- **Calldata**: This is where all incoming function execution data, including function arguments, is stored. This is a non-modifiable memory location.
- **Stack**: EVM maintains a stack for loading variables and intermediate values for working with Ethereum instruction set. This is working set memory for EVM. A stack is 1,024 levels deep in EVM and if it store anything more than this it raises an exception.

The data location of a variable is dependent on the following two factors:

- Location of variable declaration
- Data type of the variable

Based on the preceding two factors, there are rules that govern and decide the data location of a variable. The rules are mentioned here. Data locations also effect the way assignment operator works. Both assignment and data locations are explained by means of rules that govern them.

Rule 1

Variables declared as state variables are always stored in the storage data location.

Rule 2

Variables declared as function parameters are always stored in the memory data location.

Rule 3

Variables declared within functions, by default, are stored in memory data location. However, there are following few caveats:

- The location for value type variables is memory within a function while the default for a reference type variable is storage.

 Please note that storage is the default for reference type variable declared within a function. However, it can be overridden.

- By overriding the default location, reference types variables can be located at the memory data location. The reference types referred are arrays, structs, and strings.
- Reference types declared within a function without being overridden should always point to a state variable.
- Value type variables declared in a function cannot be overridden and cannot be stored at the storage location.
- Mappings are always declared at storage location. This means that they cannot be declared within a function. They cannot be declared as memory types. However, mappings in a function can refer to mappings declared as state variables.

Rule 4

Arguments supplied by callers to function parameters are always stored in a calldata data location.

Rule 5

Assignments to state variable from another state variable always creates a new copy. Two value type state variables `stateVar1` and `stateVar2` are declared. Within the `getUInt` function, `stateVar2` is assigned to `stateVar1`. At this stage, the values in both the variables are `40`. The next line of code changes the value of `stateVar2` to `50` and returns `stateVar1`. The returned value is `40` illustrating that each variable maintains its own independent value a shown in the following screenshot:

```solidity
pragma solidity 0.4.19;

contract DemoStoragetoStorageValueTypeAssignment {

    uint stateVar1 = 20;

    uint stateVar2 = 40;

    function getUInt() returns (uint)
    {
        stateVar1 = stateVar2;

        stateVar2 = 50;

        return stateVar1; // returns 40

    }

}
```

Two array type state variables, stateArray1 and stateArray2, are declared. Within the getUInt function, stateArray2 is assigned to stateArray1. At this stage, the values in both the variables are the same. The next line of code changes one of the values in stateArray2 to 5 and returns the element at same location from the stateArray1 array. The returned value is 4, illustrating that each variable maintains its own independent value as shown in the following screenshot:

```solidity
pragma solidity 0.4.19;

contract DemoStoragetoStorageReferenceTypeAssignment {

    uint[2] stateArray1 = [uint(1), 2];

    uint[2] stateArray2 = [uint(3), 4];

    function getUInt() returns (uint)
    {
      stateArray1 = stateArray2;

      stateArray2[1] = 5;

      return stateArray1[1]; // returns 4

    }
}
```

Rule 6

Assignments to storage variables from another memory variable always create a new copy.

A fixed array of uint stateArray is declared as a state variable. Within the getUInt function a local memory located fixed array of uint localArray is defined and initialized. The next line of code assigns localArray to stateArray. At this stage, the values in both the variables are the same. The next line of code changes one of the values in localArray to 10 and returns the element at same location from the stateArray1 array. The returned value is 2, illustrating that each variable maintains its own independent value as shown in the following screenshot:

```
pragma solidity 0.4.19;

contract DemoMemorytoStorageReferenceTypeAssignment {

    uint[2] stateArray ;
    function getUInt() returns (uint)
    {
      uint[2] memory localArray = [uint(1), 2];

      stateArray = localArray;

      localArray[1] = 10;

      return stateArray[1]; // returns 2

    }
}
```

A value type `stateVar` state variables is declared and initialized with value 20. Within the `getUInt` function, a `localVar` local variable is declared with value 40. In next line of code, the `localVar` local variable is assigned to `stateVar`. At this stage, the values in both the variables are 40. The next line of code changes the value of `localVar` to 50 and returns `stateVar`. The returned value is 40, illustrating that each variable maintains its own independent value as shown in the following screenshot:

```
pragma solidity 0.4.19;

contract DemoMemorytoStorageValueTypeAssignment {

    uint stateVar = 20;
    function getUInt() returns (uint)
    {
      uint localVar = 40;

      stateVar = localVar;

      localVar = 50;

      return stateVar; // returns 40

    }
}
```

Rule 7

Assignments to memory variable from another state variable always creates a new copy. A value type state variable, `stateVar` is declared and initialized with value 20. Within the `getUInt` function a local variable of type `uint` is declared and initiated with value 40. The `stateVar` variable is assigned to the `localVar` variable. At this stage, the values in both the variables are 20. The next line of code changes the value of `stateVar` to 50 and returns `localVar`. The returned value is 20, illustrating that each variable maintains its own independent value as shown in the following screenshot:

```
pragma solidity 0.4.19;

contract DemoStoragetoMemoryValueTypeAssignment {

    uint stateVar = 20;
    function getUInt() returns (uint)
    {
       uint localVar = 40;

       localVar = stateVar;

       stateVar = 50;

       return localVar; // returns 20

    }

}
```

A fixed array of uint `stateArray` is declared as state variable. Within the `getUInt` function, a local memory located, fixed array of uint `localArray` is defined and initialized with the `stateArray` variable. At this stage, the values in both the variables are the same. The next line of code changes one of the values in `stateArray` to 5 and returns the element at the same location from the `localArray1` array. The returned value is 2, illustrating that each variable maintains its own independent value as shown in the following screenshot:

```
pragma solidity 0.4.19;

contract DemoStoragetoMemoryReferenceTypeAssignment {

    uint[2] stateArray = [uint(1), 2];
    function getUInt() returns (uint)
    {
      uint[2] memory localArray = stateArray;

      stateArray[1] = 5;

      return localArray[1]; // returns 2

    }

}
```

Rule 8

Assignments to a memory variable from another memory variable do not create a copy for reference types; however, they do create a new copy for value types. The code listing shown in the following screenshot illustrates that value type variables in memory are copied by value. The value of localVar1 is not affected by change in value of the localVar2 variable:

```
pragma solidity 0.4.19;

contract DemoMemorytoMemoryValueTypeAssignment {

    function getUInt() returns (uint)
    {
      uint localVar1 = 40;

      uint localVar2 = 80;

      localVar1 = localVar2;

      localVar2 = 100;

      return localVar1; // returns 80

    }

}
```

The code listing shown in the following screenshot illustrates that reference type variables in memory are copied by reference. The value of `otherVar` is affected by change in the `someVar` variable:

```solidity
pragma solidity 0.4.19;

contract DemoMemorytoMemoryReferenceTypeAssignment {

    uint stateVar = 20;
    function getUInt() returns (uint)
    {
        uint[] memory someVar = new uint[](1);

        someVar[0] = 23;

        uint[] memory  otherVar = someVar;

        someVar[0] = 45;

        return (otherVar[0]); //returns 45

    }

}
```

Literals

Solidity provides usage of literal for assignments to variables. Literals do not have names; they are the values themselves. Variables can change their values during a program execution, but a literal remains the same value throughout. Take a look at the following examples of various literals:

- Examples of integer literal are 1, 10, 1,000, -1, and -100.
- Examples of string literals are "Ritesh" and 'Modi'. String literals can be in single or double quotes.

- Examples of address literals are 0xca35b7d915458ef540ade6068dfe2f44e8fa733c and 0x1111111111111111111111111111111111111111.
- Hexadecimal literals are prefixed with the `hex` keyword. An example of hexadecimal literals is hex"1A2B3F".
- Solidity supports decimal literals with use of dot. Examples include 4.5 and 0.2.

Integers

Integers help in storing numbers in contracts. Solidity provides the following two types of integer:

- **Signed integers**: Signed integers can hold both negative and positive values.
- **Unsigned integers**: Unsigned integers can hold only positive values along with zero. They can also hold negative values apart from positive and zero values.

There are multiple flavors of integers in Solidity for each of these types. Solidity provides uint8 type to represent 8 bit unsigned integer and thereon in multiples of 8 till it reaches 256. In short, there could be 32 different declarations of uint with different multiples of of 8, such as uint8, uint16, unit24, as far as uint256 bit. Similarly, there are equivalent data types for integers such as int8, int16 till int256.

Depending on requirements, an appropriately sized integer should be chosen. For example, while storing values between 0 and 255 uint8 is appropriate, and while storing values between -128 to 127 int8 is more suitable. For higher values, larger integers can be used.

The default value for both signed and unsigned integers is zero, to which they are initialized automatically at the time of declaration. Integers are value types; however, when used as an array they are referred as reference types.

Mathematical operations such as addition, subtraction, multiplication, division, exponential, negation, post-increment, and pre-increment can be performed on integers. The following screenshot shows some of these examples:

```solidity
pragma solidity 0.4.19;

contract AllAboutInts {


    uint   stateUInt = 20 ; //state variable
    uint   stateInt = 20 ; //state variable

    function getUInt(uint incomingValue)
    {
        uint memoryuint = 256 ;
        uint256 memoryuint256 = 256 ;
        uint8 memoryuint8 = 8 ; //can store value from 0 upto 255

        //addition of two uint8
        uint256 result = memoryuint8 + memoryuint ;

        // assignAfterIncrement = 9 and memoryuint8 = 9
        uint8 assignAfterIncrement = ++memoryuint8 ;

        // assignAfterIncrement = 9 and memoryuint8 = 10
        uint8 assignBeforeIncrement = memoryuint8++;


    }

    function getInt(int incomingValue)
    {
        int memoryInt = 256 ;
        int256 memoryInt256 = 256 ;
        int8 memoryInt8 = 8 ; //can store value from -128 to 127
    }
}
```

Boolean

Solidity, like any programming language, provides a boolean data type. The `bool` data type can be used to represent scenarios that have binary results, such as `true` or `false`, 1 or 0, and so on. The valid values for this data type are `true` and `false`. It is to be noted that bools in Solidity cannot be converted to integers, as they can in other programming languages. It's a value type and any assignment to other boolean variables creates a new copy. The default value for `bool` in Solidity is `false`.

A `bool` data type is declared and assigned a value as shown in the following code:

```
bool isPaid = true;
```

It can be modified within contracts and can be used in both incoming and outgoing parameters and the return value, as shown in the following screenshot:

```
pragma solidity 0.4.19;

contract boolContract {

    bool isPaid = true;

    function manageBool() returns (bool)
    {
        isPaid = false;

        return isPaid; //returns false
    }

    function convertToUint() returns (uint8)
    {
        isPaid = false;

        return uint8(isPaid); //error
    }
}
```

The byte data type

Byte refers to 8 bit signed integers. Everything in memory is stored in bits consisting of binary values—0 and 1. Solidity also provides the byte data type to store information in binary format. Generally, programming languages have a single data type for representing bytes. However, Solidity has multiple flavors of the byte type. It provides data types in the range from bytes1 to bytes32 inclusive, to represent varying byte lengths, as required. These are called **fixed sized byte arrays** and are implemented as value types. The bytes1 data type represents 1 byte and bytes2 represents 2 bytes. The default value for byte is 0x00 and it gets initialized with this value. Solidity also has a byte type that is an alias to bytes1.

A byte can be assigned byte values in hexadecimal format, as follows:

```
bytes1 aa = 0x65;
```

A byte can be assigned integer values in decimal format, as follows:

```
bytes1 bb = 10;
```

A byte can be assigned negative integer values in decimal format, as follows:

```
bytes1 ee = -100;
```

A byte can be assigned character values as follows:

```
bytes1 dd = 'a';
```

In the following code snippet, a value of 256 cannot fit in a single byte and needs a bigger byte array:

```
bytes2 cc = 256;
```

The code listing in the following screenshot shows how to store binary, positive, and negative integers, and character literals in fixed sized byte arrays.

We can also perform bitwise operations such as and, or, xor, not, and left and right shift operations on the byte data type:

```solidity
pragma solidity 0.4.19;

contract bytesContract {

    bytes1 aa = 0x65;
    bytes1 bb = 10;
    bytes2 cc = 256;
    bytes1 dd = 'a';
    bytes1 ee = -100;

    function getintaa() returns (uint)
    {
      return uint(aa); //returns 101
    }

    function getbyteaa() returns (bytes1)
    {
      return aa; //returns 0x65
    }

    function getbytebb() returns (bytes1)
    {
      return bb; //returns 0x0a
    }

    function getintbb() returns (uint)
    {
      return uint(bb); //returns 10
    }

    function getbytecc() returns (bytes2)
    {
      return cc; //returns 0x0100
    }

    function getintcc() returns (uint)
    {
      return uint(cc); //returns 256
    }

    function getbytedd() returns (bytes2)
    {
      return dd; //returns 0x6100 or 0x61 for bytes1
    }

    function getintdd() returns (uint)
    {
      return uint(dd); //returns 97
    }
}
```

Arrays

Arrays are discussed as data types but, more specifically they are data structures that are dependent on other data types. Arrays refer to groups of values of the same type. Arrays help in storing these values together and ease the process of iterating, sorting, and searching for individuals or subsets of elements within this group. Solidity provides rich array constructs that cater to different needs.

An example of an array in Solidity is as follows:

```
uint[5] intArray ;
```

Arrays in Solidity can be fixed or dynamic.

Fixed arrays

Fixed arrays refer to arrays that have a pre-determined size mentioned at declaration. Examples of fixed arrays are as follows:

```
int[5] age ; // array of int with 5 fixed storage space allocated
byte[4] flags ; // array of byte with 4 fixed storage space allocated
```

Fixed arrays cannot be initialized using the new keyword. They can only be initialized inline, as shown in the following code:

```
int[5] age = [int(10), 20,30,40,50] ;
```

They can also be initialized inline within a function later, as follows:

```
int[5] age ;
age = [int(10),2,3,4,5];
```

Dynamic arrays

Dynamic arrays refer to arrays that do not have a pre-determined size at the time of declaration; however, their size is determined at runtime. Take a look at the following code:

```
int[] age ; // array of int with no fixed storage space allocated. Storage
is allocated during assignment
byte[] flags ; // array of byte with no fixed storage space allocated
```

Dynamic arrays can be initialized inline or using the new operator. The initialization can happen at the time of declaration as follows:

```
int[] age = [int(10), 20,30,40,50] ;
int[] age = new int[](5) ;
```

The initialization can also happen within a function later in the following two different steps:

```
int[] age ;
age = new int[](5) ;
```

Special arrays

Solidity provides the following two special arrays:

- The bytes array
- The String array

The bytes array

The bytes array is a dynamic array that can hold any number of bytes. It is not the same as byte []. The byte [] array takes 32 bytes for each element whereas bytes tightly holds all the bytes together.

Bytes can be declared as a state variable with initial length size as shown in the following code:

```
bytes localBytes = new bytes(0) ;
```

This can be also divided into the following two code lines similar to previously discussed arrays:

```
bytes localBytes ;
localBytes= new bytes (10) ;
```

Bytes can be assigned values directly, as follows:

```
localBytes = "Ritesh Modi";
```

Also, values can be pushed into it, as shown in the following code, if it is located at the storage location:

```
localBytes.push(byte(10));
```

Bytes also provide a read/write `length` property, as follows:

```
return localBytes.length; //reading the length property
```

Take a look at the following code as well:

```
localBytes.length = 4; //setting bytes length to 4 bytes
```

The String array

Strings are dynamic data types that are based on bytes arrays discussed in the previous section. They are very similar to bytes with additional constraints. Strings cannot be indexed or pushed and do not have the `length` property. To perform any of these actions on string variables, they should first be converted into bytes and then converted back to strings after the operation.

Strings can be composed of characters within single or double quotes.

Strings can be declared and assigned values directly, as follows:

```
String name = 'Ritesh Modi" ;
```

They can be also converted to bytes, as follows:

```
Bytes byteName = bytes(name) ;
```

Array properties

There are basic properties supported by arrays. In Solidity, due to the multiple types of array, not every type supports all of these properties.

These properties are as follows:

- index: This property used for reading individual array elements is supported by all types of arrays, except for the string type. The index property for writing to individual array element is supported for dynamic arrays, fixed arrays, and the bytes type only. Writing is not supported for string and fixed sized byte arrays.
- push: This property is supported by dynamic arrays only.
- length: This property is supported by all arrays from read perspective, except for the string type. Only dynamic arrays and bytes support modifying the length property.

Structure of an array

We have already briefly touched on the topic of structures. Structures help in defining custom user-defined data structures. Structures help in group multiple variables of different data types into a single type. A structure does not contain any programming logic or code for execution; it just contains a variable declaration. Structures are reference types and are treated as complex type in Solidity.

Structures can be defined as state variables, as shown in the next code illustration. A struct composed of string, uint, bool, and uint arrays is defined. There are two state variables. They are on the storage location. While the first stateStructure1 state variable is initialized at the time of declaration, the other stateStructure1 state variable is left to be initialized later within a function.

A local structure at the memory location is declared and initialized within the getAge function.

Another structure is declared that acts as a pointer to the stateStructure state variable.

A third local structure is declared that refers to the previously created localStructure local structure.

A change in one of the properties of `localStructure` is performed while the previously declared state structure is initialized and finally the age from `pointerLocalStructure` is returned. It returns the new value that was assigned to `localStructure`, as shown in the following screenshot:

```solidity
pragma solidity 0.4.19;

//contract definition
contract generalStructure {
    //state variables

    //structure definition
    struct myStruct {
        string name; //variable fo type string
        uint myAge; // variable of unsigned integer type
        bool isMarried; // variable of boolean type
        uint[] bankAccountsNumbers; // variable - dynamic array of unsigned integer
    }

    // state structure
    myStruct  stateStructure = myStruct("Ritesh", 10, true, new uint[](2));

    myStruct  stateStructure1;


    //function definition
    function getAge ()  returns (uint) {

        // local structure
        myStruct memory localStructure = myStruct("Modi", 20 ,false, new uint[](2));

        //local pointer to State structure
        myStruct pointerStructure = stateStructure;

        // pointerlocalStructure is reference to localStructure
        myStruct memory pointerlocalStructure = localStructure;

        //changing value in localStructure
        localStructure.myAge = 30;

        //assigning values to state variable
        stateStructure1 =   myStruct("Ritesh", 10, true, new uint[](2));

        //returning pointerlocalStructure.Age -- returns 30
        return pointerlocalStructure.myAge;

    }
}
```

Enumerations

We have briefly touched on the concept of enumerations while discussing the layout of the Solidity file earlier in this chapter. Enums are value types comprising a pre-defined list of constant values. They are passed by values and each copy maintains its own value. Enums cannot be declared within functions and are declared within the global namespace of the contract.

Predefined constants are assigned consecutively, increasing integer values starting from zero.

The code illustration shown next declares an enum identified as a status consisting of five constant values—created, approved, provisioned, rejected, and deleted. They have integer values 0, 1, 2, 3, 4 assigned to them.

A instance of enum named myStatus is created with an initial value of provisioned.

The returnEnum function returns the status and it returns the integer value. It is to be noted that web3 and **Decentralized Applications (DApp)** do not understand an enum declared within a contract. They will get an integer value corresponding to the enum constant.

The returnEnumInt function returns an integer value.

The passByValue function shows that the enum instance maintains its own local copy and does not share with other instances.

The `assignInteger` function shows an example where an integer is assigned as a value to an `enum` instance:

```
pragma solidity 0.4.19;

contract Enums {

//enum declared
enum status {created, approved, provisioned, rejected, deleted}

//instance of enum with initial value 2
status myStatus = status.provisioned;

    function returnEnum() returns (status)
    {
        status stat = status.created;
        return stat;
    }

    function returnEnumInt() returns (uint)
    {

        status stat = status.approved;
        return uint(stat);
    }

    function passByValue() returns (uint)
    {

        status stat = myStatus;
        myStatus = status.rejected;

        return uint(myStatus);
    }

    function assignInteger() returns (uint)
    {

        status stat = myStatus;

        //casting integer 2 to enum and assigning
        myStatus = status(2);

        return uint(myStatus);
    }
}
```

Address

An address is a 20 bytes data type. It is specifically designed to hold account addresses in Ethereum, which are 160 bits or 20 bytes in size. It can hold contract account addresses as well as externally owned account addresses. Address is a value type and it creates a new copy while being assigned to another variable.

Address has a `balance` property that returns the amount of Ether available with the account and has a few functions for transferring Ether to accounts and invoking contract functions.

It provides the following two functions to transfer Ether:

- `transfer`
- `send`

The `transfer` function is a better alternative for transferring Ether to an account than the `send` function. The `send` function returns a boolean value depending on successful execution of the Ether transfer while the `transfer` function raises an exception and returns the Ether to the caller.

It also provides the following three functions for invoking the `contract` function:

- `Call`
- `DelegateCall`
- `Callcode`

Mappings

Mappings are one of the most used complex data types in Solidity. Mappings are similar to hash tables or dictionaries in other languages. They help in storing key-value pairs and enable retrieving values based on the supplied key.

Mappings are declared using the `mapping` keyword followed by data types for both key and value separated by the `=>` notation. Mappings have identifiers like any other data type and they can be used to access the mapping.

An example of mapping is as follows:

```
Mapping ( uint => address ) Names ;
```

In the preceding code, the `uint` data type is used for storing the keys and the `address` data type is used for storing the values. `Names` is used as an identifier for the mapping.

Although it is similar to a hash table and dictionary, Solidity does not allow iterating through mapping. A value from mapping can be retrieved if the key is known. The next example illustrates working with mapping. A counter of type `uint` is maintained in a contract that acts as a key and address details are stored and retrieved with the help of functions.

To access any particular value in mapping, the associated key should be used along with the mapping name as shown here:

```
Names[counter]
```

To store a value in mapping, use the following syntax:

```
Names[counter] = <<some value>>
```

Take a look at the following screenshot:

```solidity
pragma solidity 0.4.19;

contract GeneralMapping {

    mapping (uint => address) Names;

    uint counter;

    function addtoMapping(address addressDetails) returns (uint)
    {
        counter = counter + 1;
      Names[counter] = addressDetails;

      return counter; //returns false
    }

    function getMappingMember(uint id) returns (address)
    {
      return Names[id];
    }
}
```

Although mapping doesn't support iteration, there are ways to work round this limitation. The next example illustrates one of the ways to iterate through mapping. Please note that iterating and looping are an expensive operation in Ethereum in terms of gas usage and should generally be avoided. In this example, a separate counter is maintained to keep track of the number of entries stored within the mapping. This counter also acts as the key within the mapping. A local array can be constructed for storing the values from mapping. A loop can be executed using `counter` and can extract and store each value from the mapping into the local array as shown in the following screenshot:

```solidity
pragma solidity 0.4.19;

contract MappingLooping {

    mapping (uint => address) Names;

    uint counter;

    function addtoMapping(address addressDetails) returns (uint)
    {
      counter = counter + 1;

      Names[counter] = addressDetails;

      return counter;
    }

    function getMappingMember(uint id) returns (address[])
    {
      address[] memory localBytes = new address[](counter);
      for(uint i=1; i<= counter; i++){
          localBytes[i - 1] = Names[i];
      }

      return localBytes;
    }
}
```

Mapping can only be declared as a state variable whose memory location is of type storage. Mapping cannot be declared within functions as memory mappings. However, mappings can be declared in functions if they refer to mappings declared in state variables, as shown in the following example:

```solidity
Mapping (uint => address) localNames = Names ;
```

This is valid syntax as the `localNames` mapping is referring to the `Names` state variable:

```
pragma solidity 0.4.19;

contract MappinginMemory {

    mapping (uint => address) Names;

    uint counter;

    function addtoMapping(address addressDetails) returns (uint)
    {
      counter = counter + 1;
      mapping (uint => address) localNames = Names;

      localNames[counter] = addressDetails;

      return counter;
    }
    function getMappingMember(uint id) returns (address)
    {
      return Names[id];
    }
}
```

It is also possible to have nested mapping, that is mapping consisting of mappings. The next example illustrates this. In this example, there is an apparent mapping that maps `uint` to another mapping. The child mapping is stored as a value for the first mapping. The child mapping has the `address` type as the key and the `string` type as value. There is a single mapping identifier and the child or inner mapping can be accessed using this identifier itself as shown in the following code:

```
mapping (uint => mapping(address => string)) accountDetails;
```

To add an entry to this type of nested mapping, the following syntax can be used:

```
accountDetails[counter][addressDetails] = names;
```

Here, `accountDetails` is the mapping identifier and `counter` is the key for parent mapping. The `accountDetails[counter]` mapping identifier retrieves the value from the parent mapping, which in turn happens to be another mapping. Adding the key to the returned value, we can set the value for the inner mapping. Similarly, the value from the inner mapping can be retrieved using the following syntax:

```
accountDetails[counter][addressDetails]
```

Take a look at the following screenshot:

```
pragma solidity 0.4.19;

contract DemoInnerMapping {

    mapping (uint => mapping(address => string)) accountDetails;
    uint counter;

    function addtoMapping(address addressDetails, bytes name) returns (uint)
    {
        string memory names = string(name);
        counter = counter + 1;
        accountDetails[counter][addressDetails] = names;

        return counter;
    }

    function getMappingMember(address addressDetails) returns (bytes)
    {
        // 0xca35b7d915458ef540ade6068dfe2f44e8fa733c
      return bytes( accountDetails[counter][addressDetails]);
    }
}
```

Summary

This is the first chapter that has explored Solidity in depth. This chapter introduced Solidity, the layout of Solidity files including elements that can be declared at the top level in it. Constructs li pragma, contracts, and elements of contracts were discussed for a layout perspective. A complete immersion into the world of Solidity data types forms the core of this chapter. Value types and reference types were discussed in depth along with types like int, uint, fixed sized byte arrays, bytes, arrays, strings, structures, enumerations, addresses, boolean, and mappings were discussed in great length along with examples. Solidity provides additional data locations from complex types such as structs and arrays, which were also discussed in depth along with rules that govern their usage.

In the next chapter, we will focus on using some out-of-box variables and functions of smart contracts. Solidity provides numerous global variables and functions to help ease the task of obtaining the current transaction and block context. These variables and function provides contextual information and Solidity code and utilizes them for logic execution. They play a very important role in authoring enterprise-scale smart contracts.

Global Variables and Functions

In `Chapter 3`, *Introducing Solidity*, you learned about Solidity data types in detail. Data types can be value or reference types. Some reference types such as structs and arrays also have data locations—memory and storage associated with them. Variables could be state variables or variables defined locally within functions. This chapter will focus on variables, their scoping rules, declaration and initialization, conversion rules hoisting, and variables available globally to all contracts. Some global functions will also be discussed in this chapter.

We will cover the following topics in this chapter:

- The `var` data type
- Variable scoping
- Variable conversion
- Variable hoisting
- Block related global variables
- Transaction related global variables
- Mathematical and cryptographic global functions
- Addressing related global variables and functions
- Contract-related global variables and functions

The var type variables

One Solidity type that was not discussed in the last chapter is the `var` data type. `var` is a special type that can only be declared within a function. There cannot be a state variable in a contract of type `var`. Variables declared with the `var` type are known as **implicitly typed variable** because `var` does not represent any type explicitly. It informs the compiler that its type is dependent and determined by the value assigned to it the first time. Once a type is determined, it cannot be changed.

The compiler decides the final data type for the var variables instead of a developer mentioning the type. It is therefore quite possible that the type determined by the block.difficulty (uint) current block compiler might not exactly be the type expected by code execution. var cannot be used with the explicit usage of memory location. An explicit memory location needs an explicit variable type.

An example of var is shown in the following screenshot. Variable uintVar8 is of type uint8, variable uintVar16 is of type uint16, variable intVar8 is of type int8 (signed integer), variable intVar16 is of type int16 (signed integer), variable boolVar is of type bool, variable stringVar is of type string, variable bytesVar is of type bytes, variable arrayInteger is of type uint8 array, and variable arrayByte is of type bytes10 array:

```
pragma solidity 0.4.19;

contract VarExamples {

    function VarType()
    {
        var uintVar8 = 10; //uint8
        uintVar8 = 255; //256 is error

        var uintVar16 = 256; //uint16
        uintVar16 = 65535; //aaa = 65536; is error

        var intVar8 = -1; //int8 values -128 to 127

        var intVar16 = -129; //int16 values -32768 to 32767

        var boolVar = true;
        boolVar = false; // 10 is error, 0 is error, 1 is error, -1 is error

        var stringVar = "0x10"; // this is string memory
        stringVar = "10"; // cc =123123123123123123123121212222222 is error

        var bytesVar = 0x100; // this is byte memory

        var Var = hex"001122FF";

        var arrayInteger = [uint8(1),2];
        arrayInteger[1] = 255;

        var arrayByte = bytes10(0x2222);
        arrayByte = 0x11111111111111111111; //0x11111111111111111111111 is error

    }
}
```

Variables hoisting

Hoisting a concept is where variables need not be declared and initialized before using the variable. The variable declaration can happen at any place within a function, even after using it. This is known as **variable hoisting**. The Solidity compiler extracts all variables declared anywhere within a function and places them at the top or beginning of a function and we all know that declaring a variable in Solidity also initializes them with their respective default values. This ensures that the variables are available throughout the function.

In the following example, `firstVar`, `secondVar`, and `result` are declared towards the end of the function but utilized at the beginning of the function. However, when the compiler generates the bytecode for the contract, it declares all variables as the first set of instructions in a function as shown in the following screenshot:

```solidity
pragma solidity ^0.4.19;

contract variableHoisting {

    function hoistingDemo() returns (uint){

        firstVar = 10;
        secondVar = 20;

        result = firstVar + secondVar;

        uint firstVar;
        uint secondVar;
        uint result;
        return result;


    }

}
```

Variable scoping

Scoping refers to the availability of a variable within a function and a contract in Solidity. Solidity provides the following two locations where variables can be declared:

- Contract-level global variables—also known as state variables
- Function-level local variables

It is quite easy to understand function-level local variables. They are only available anywhere within a function and not outside.

Contract-level global variables are variables that are available to all functions including constructor, fallback, and modifiers within a contract. Contract-level global variables can have a visibility modifier attached to them. It is important to understand that state data can be viewed across the entire network irrespective of the visibility modifier. The following state variables can only be modified using functions:

- `public`: These state variables are accessible directly from external calls. A `getter` function is implicitly generated by the compiler to read the value of public state variables.
- `internal`: These state variables are not accessible directly from external calls. They are accessible from functions within a current contract and child contracts deriving from it.
- `private`: These state variables are not accessible directly from external calls. They are also not accessible from functions from child contracts. They are only accessible from functions within the current contract.

Let's take a look at the preceding state variables in the following screenshot:

```
pragma solidity ^0.4.19;

contract ScopingDtateVariables {

//    uint64 public myVar = 0;

//    uint64 private myVar = 0;

//    uint64 internal myVar = 0;


}
```

Type conversion

By now, we know that Solidity is a statically typed language, where variables are defined with specific data types at compile time. The data type cannot be changed for the lifetime of the variable. It means it can only store values that are legal for a data type. For example, uint8 can store values from 0 to 255. It cannot store negative values or values greater than 255. Take a look at the following code to better understand this:

```solidity
pragma solidity ^0.4.19;

contract ErrorDataType {

    function hostingDemo() returns (uint){

        uint8 someVar = 100;
        someVar = 300; //error


    }
}
```

However, there are times when these conversions are required to copy a value into a variable of one type to another, and these are called **type conversions**. Solidity provides rules for type conversions.

In Solidity, we can perform various kinds of conversion and we will cover these in the following sections.

Implicit conversion

Implicit conversion means that there is no need for an operator, or no external help is required for conversion. These types of conversion are perfectly legal and there is no loss of data or mismatch of values. They are completely type-safe. Solidity allows for implicit conversion from smaller to larger integral types. For example, converting uint8 to uint16 happens implicitly.

Explicit conversion

Explicit conversion is required when a compiler does not perform implicit conversion either because of loss of data or a value containing data not falling within a target data type range. Solidity provides a function for each value type for explicit conversion. Examples of explicit conversion are `uint16` conversion to `uint8`. Data loss is possible in such cases.

The following code listing shows examples for both implicit and explicit conversions:

- `ConvertionExplicitUINT8toUINT256`: This function executed explicit conversion from `uint8` to `uint256`. It is to be noted that this conversion was also possible implicitly.
- `ConvertionExplicitUINT256toUINT8`: This function executed explicit conversion from `uint256` to `uint8`. This conversion will raise a compile time error if the conversion happened implicitly.
- `ConvertionExplicitUINT256toUINT81`: This function shows an interesting aspect of explicit conversion. Explicit conversions are error-prone and should generally be avoided. In this function, an attempt is made to store a large value in a variable of a smaller data type. This results in loss of data and unpredictability. The compiler does not generate an error; however, it tries to fit the value into smaller value and goes in cycle to find a valid value.
- `Conversions`: This function shows an example of implicit and explicit conversions. Some fail and some are legal. In the following screenshot, please read the comments beneath the code to understand them:

```solidity
pragma solidity ^0.4.19;

contract ConversionDemo {

    function ConvertionExplicitUINT8toUINT256() returns (uint){
        uint8 myVariable = 10;
        uint256 someVariable = myVariable;
        return someVariable;
    }

    function ConvertionExplicitUINT256toUINT8() returns (uint8){
        uint256 myVariable = 10;
        uint8 someVariable = uint8(myVariable);
        return someVariable;
    }

    function ConvertionExplicitUINT256toUINT81() returns (uint8){
        uint256 myVariable = 10000134;
        uint8 someVariable = uint8(myVariable);
        return someVariable; //returns 6 as return value
    }

    function Convertions() {

        uint256 myVariable = 10000134;
        uint8 someVariable   = 100;
        bytes4 byte4 = 0x65666768;

        // bytes1 byte1 = 0x656667668; //error

        bytes1 byte1 = 0x65;

        //  byte1 = byte4; //error, explicit conversion needed here

        byte1 = bytes1(byte4) ; //explicit conversion

        byte4 = byte1;  //Implicit conversion

        // uint8 someVariable = myVariable; // error, explicit conversion needed here

        myVariable = someVariable; //Implicit conversion

        string memory name = "Ritesh";
        bytes memory nameInBytes = bytes(name); //explicit string to bytes conversion

        name = string(nameInBytes); //explicit bytes to string conversion

    }
}
```

Block and transaction global variables

Solidity provides access to a few global variables that are not declared within contracts but are accessible from code within contracts. Contracts cannot access the ledger directly. A ledger is maintained by miners only; however Solidity provides some information about the current transaction and block to contracts so that they can utilize them. Solidity provides both block-as well as transaction-related variables.

The following code illustratesexamples of using global transaction, block, and message variables:

```solidity
pragma solidity ^0.4.19;

contract TransactionAndMessageVariables {

    event logstring(string);
    event loguint(uint);
    event logbytes(bytes);
    event logaddress(address);
    event logbyte4(bytes4);
    event logblock(bytes32);

    function globalVariable() payable {

        logaddress( block.coinbase ); // 0x94d76e24f818426ae84aa404140e8d5f60e10e7e

        loguint( block.difficulty ); //71762765929000

        loguint( block.gaslimit ); // 6000000

        loguint(  msg.gas ); //2975428

        loguint(  tx.gasprice ); // 1

        loguint(  block.number ); //123

        loguint( block.timestamp ); //1513061946

        loguint( now ); //1513061946

        logbytes( msg.data ); // 0x4048d797

        logbyte4(   msg.sig ); // // 0x4048d797

        loguint( msg.value ); // 0 or in Wei if ether are send

        logaddress( msg.sender ); //0xca35b7d915458ef540ade6068dfe2f44e8fa733c"

        logaddress( tx.origin ); // 0xca35b7d915458ef540ade6068dfe2f44e8fa733c"

        logblock ( block.blockhash( block.number) ); //0x0000000000000000000000000

    }
}
```

Transaction and message global variables

The following is a list of global variables along with their data types and a description provided as a ready reference:

Variable name	Description
`block.coinbase (address)`	Same as etherbase. Refers to the miner's address.
`block.difficulty (uint)`	Difficulty level of current block.
`block.gaslimit (uint)`	Gas limit for current block.
`block.number (uint)`	Block number in sequence.
`block.timestamp (uint)`	Time when block was created.
`msg.data (bytes)`	Information about the function and its parameters that created the transaction.
`msg.gas (uint)`	Gas unused after execution of transaction.
`msg.sender (address)`	Address of caller who invoked the function.
`msg.sig (bytes4)`	Function identifier using first four bytes after hashing function signature.
`msg.value (uint)`	Amount of wei sent along with transaction.
`now (uint)`	Current time.
`tx.gasprice (uint)`	The gas price caller is ready to pay for each gas unit.
`tx.origin (address)`	The first caller of the transaction.
`block.blockhash(uint blockNumber) returns (bytes32)`	Hash of the block containing the transaction.

Difference between tx.origin and msg.sender

Careful readers might have noticed in the previous code illustration that both tx.origin and msg.sender show the same result and output. The tx.origin global variable refers to the original external account that started the transaction while msg.sender refers to the immediate account (it could be external or another contract account) that invokes the function. The tx.origin variable will always refer to the external account while msg.sender can be a contract or external account. If there are multiple function invocations on multiple contracts, tx.origin will always refer to the account that started the transaction irrespective of the stack of contracts invoked. However, msg.sender will refer to the immediate previous account (contract/external) that invokes the next contract. It is recommended to use msg.sender over tx.origin.

Cryptography global variables

Solidity provides cryptographic functions for hashing values within contract functions. There are two hashing functions—SHA2 and SHA3.

The sha3 function converts the input into a hash based on the sha3 algorithm while sha256 converts the input into a hash based on the sha2 algorithm. There is another function, keccak256, which is an alias of the SHA3 algorithm. It is recommended to use the keccak256 or sha3 functions for hashing needs.

The following screenshot of the code segment illustrates this:

```solidity
pragma solidity ^0.4.19;

contract CryptoFunctions {

    function cryptoDemo() returns (bytes32, bytes32, bytes32){

        return (sha256("r"), keccak256("r"), sha3("r"));


    }

}
```

The result of executing this function is shown in the following screenshot. The result of both the `keccak256` and `sha3` functions is the same:

```
{
    "0": "bytes32: 0x454349e422f05297191ead13e21d3db520e5abef52055e4964b82fb213f593a1",
    "1": "bytes32: 0x414f72a4d550cad29f17d9d99a4af64b3776ec5538cd440cef0f03fef2e9e010",
    "2": "bytes32: 0x414f72a4d550cad29f17d9d99a4af64b3776ec5538cd440cef0f03fef2e9e010"
}
```

All three of these functions work on tightly packed arguments, meaning that multiple parameters can be concatenated together to find a hash, as shown in the following code snippet:

```
keccak256(97, 98, 99)
```

Address global variables

Every address—externally owned or contract-based, has five global functions and a single global variable. These functions and variables will be explored in depth in subsequent chapters on Solidify functions. The global variable related to the address is called **balance** and it provides the current balance of Ether in wei available at the address.

The functions are as follows:

- `<address>.transfer(uint256 amount)`: This function sends the given amount of wei to `address`, throws on failure
- `<address>.send(uint256 amount) returns (bool)`: This function sends the given amount of wei to `address`, and returns `false` on failure
- `<address>.call(...) returns (bool)`: This function issues a low-level `call`, and returns `false` on failure
- `<address>.callcode(...) returns (bool)`: This function issues a low-level `callcode`, and returns `false` on failure
- `<address>.delegatecall(...) returns (bool)`: This function issues a low-level `delegatecall`, and returns `false` on failure

Contract global variables

Every contract has the following three global functions:

- `this`: The current contract's type, explicitly convertible to address
- `selfdestruct`: This is an address recipient that destroys the current contract, sending its funds to the given address
- `suicide`: This is an address recipient too alias to `selfdestruct`

Summary

This chapter, in many ways, was a continuation of previous chapters. Variables were discussed in depth in the first half of this chapter. Variable hoisting, type conversions, details about the `var` data type, and the scope of Solidity variables were elaborated on, along with code examples. The latter half of the chapter focused on globally available variables and functions. Transaction and message related variables, such as `block.coinbase`, `msg.data` and many more, were explained. The difference between `msg.sender` and `tx.origin` along with their usage was also explained in this chapter. This chapter also discussed cryptographic, address, and contract-level functions. However, we will focus on these functions in another chapter later in this book.

The following chapter will focus on Solidity expressions and control structures, covering programming details about loops and conditions. This will be an important chapter because every program needs some kind of looping to perform repetitive tasks and Solidity control structures help implement these. Loops are based on conditions and conditions are written using expressions. These expressions are evaluated and return either `true` or `false`. Stay tuned while we plunge into control structures and expressions in the following chapter.

5
Expressions and Control Structures

Taking decisions in code is an important aspect of a programming language, and Solidity should also be able to execute different instructions based on circumstances. Solidity provides the `if...else` and `switch` statements for this purpose. It is also important to loop through multiple items and Solidity provides multiple constructs such as `for` loops and `while` statements for this purpose. In this chapter, we will discuss in detail the programming constructs that help you take decisions and loop through a set of values.

This chapter covers the following topics:

- Expressions
- The `if...else` statement
- The `while` statement
- The `for` loop
- The `break` and `continue` keywords
- The `return` statement

Solidity expressions

An expression refers to a statement (comprising multiple operands and optionally zero or more operators) that results in a single value, object, or function. The operand can be a literal, variable, function invocation, or another expression itself.

An example of an expression is as follows:

```
Age > 10
```

In the preceding code, `Age` is a variable and `10` is an integer literal. `Age` and `10` are operands and the (>) greater than symbol is the operator. This expression returns a single boolean value (`true` or `false`) depending on the value stored in `Age`.

Expressions can be more complex comprising multiple operands and operators, as follows:

```
((Age > 10) && (Age < 20) ) || ((Age > 40) && (Age < 50) )
```

In the preceding code, there are multiple operators in play. The `&&` operator acts as an AND operator between two expressions, which in turn comprises operands and operators. There is also an OR operator represented by the `||` operator between two complex expressions.

Solidity has the following comparison operators that help in writing expressions returning Boolean values:

Operator	Meaning	Sample example
==	Equals	`myVar == 10`
!=	Not equals	`myVar != 10`
>	Greater than	`myVar > 10`
<	Less than	`myVar < 10`
>=	Greater than or equal to	`myVar >= 10`
<=	Less than or equal to	`myVar <= 10`

Solidity also provides the following logical operators that help in writing expressions returning Boolean values:

Operator	Meaning	Sample example
&&	AND	`( myVar > 10) && (myVar < 10)`
||	OR	`myVar != 10`
!	NOT	`myVar > 10`

The following operators have precedence in Solidity just like other languages:

Precedence	Description	Operator
1	Postfix increment and decrement	`++`, `--`
New expression	`new <typename>`	NA
Array subscripting	`<array>[<index>]`	NA
Member access	`<object>.<member>`	NA
Function-like call	`<func>(<args...>)`	NA
Parentheses	`(<statement>)`	NA
2	Prefix increment and decrement	`++`, `--`
Unary plus and minus	`+`, `-`	NA
Unary operations	`delete`	NA
Logical NOT	`!`	NA
Bitwise NOT	`~`	NA
3	Exponentiation	`**`
4	Multiplication, division, and modulo	`*`, `/`, `%`
5	Addition and subtraction	`+`, `-`
6	Bitwise shift operators	`<<`, `>>`
7	Bitwise AND	`&`
8	Bitwise XOR	`^`
9	Bitwise OR	`|`
10	Inequality operators	`<, >, <=, >=`
11	Equality operators	`==, !=`
12	Logical AND	`&&`
13	Logical OR	`||`
14	Ternary operator	`<conditional> ? <if-true> : <if-false>`

15	Assignment operators	$=$, $\vert=$, $\wedge=$, $\&=$, $<<=$, $>>=$, $+=$, $-=$, $*=$, $/=$, $\%=$
16	Comma operator	,

The if decision control

Solidity provides conditional code execution with the help of the `if...else` instructions. The general structure of `if...else` is as follows:

```
if (this condition/expression is true) {
    Execute the instructions here
}
else if (this condition/expression is true) {
    Execute the instructions here
}
else {
    Execute the instructions here
}
```

`if` and `if-else` are keywords in Solidity and they inform the compiler that they contain a decision control condition, for example, `if (a > 10)`. Here, `if` contains a condition that can evaluate to either `true` or `false`. If `a > 10` evaluates to `true` then the code instructions that follow in the pair of double-brackets (`{`) and (`}`) should be executed.

`else` is also a keyword that provides an alternate path if none of the previous conditions are true. It also contains a decision control instruction and executes the code instructions if `a > 10` tends to be `true`.

The following example shows the usage of 'IF'-'ELSE IF' - 'ELSE' conditions. An `enum` with multiple constants is declared. A `StateManagement` function accepts an `uint8` argument, which is converted into an `enum` constant and compared within the `if...else` decision control structure. If the value is 1 then the returned result is 1; if the argument contains 2 or 3 as value, then the `else...if` portion of code gets executed; and if the value is other than 1,2, or 3 then the else part is executed:

```
pragma solidity ^0.4.19;

contract IfElseExample {

    enum requestState {created, approved, provisioned, rejected, deleted, none}

    function StateManagement(uint8 _state) returns (int result) {

        requestState currentState = requestState(_state);

        if(currentState == requestState(1)){
            result = 1;
        } else if ((currentState == requestState.approved) || (currentState == requestState.provisioned)) {
            result = 2;
        } else {
            currentState == requestState.none;
            result = 3;
        }

    }
}
```

The while loop

There are times when we need to execute a code segment repeatedly based on a condition. Solidity provides `while` loops precisely for this purpose. The general form of the `while` loop is as follows:

```
Declare and initialize a counter
while (check the value of counter using an expression or condition) {
    Execute the instructions here
    Increment the value of counter
}
```

`while` is a keyword in Solidity and it informs the compiler that it contains a decision control instruction. If this expression evaluates to true then the code instructions that follow in the pair of double-brackets { and } should be executed. The `while` loop keeps executing until the condition turns false.

In the following example, `mapping` is declared along with `counter`. `counter` helps loop the `mapping` since there is no out-of-the-box support in Solidity to loop `mapping`.

An event is used to get details about transaction information. We will discuss events in detail in the *Events and Logging* section in `Chapter 8`, *Exceptions, Events, and Logging*. For now, it is enough to understand that you are logging information whenever an event is invoked. The `SetNumber` function adds data to mapping and the `getnumbers` function runs a `while` loop to retrieve all entries within the mapping and log them using events.

 A temporary variable is used as a counter that is incremented by 1 at every execution of the `while` loop.

The `while` condition checks the value of the temporary variable and compares it with the global counter variable. Based on whether it's true or false, the code within the `while` loop is executed. Within this set of instructions, the value of a counter should be modified so that it can help to exit the loop by making the `while` condition false as shown in the following screenshot:

```solidity
pragma solidity ^0.4.19;

contract whileLoop {

    mapping (uint => uint) blockNumber;
    uint counter;

    event uintNumber(uint);
    bytes aa;

    function SetNumber()  {
        blockNumber[counter++] = block.number;
    }

    function getNumbers() {
        uint i = 0;
        while (i < counter) {
            uintNumber( blockNumber[i]  );
            i = i + 1;
        }

    }
}
```

The for loop

One of the most famous and most used loops is the `for` loop, and we can use it in Solidity. The general structure of a `for` loop is as follows:

```
for (initialize loop counter; check and test the counter; increase the
value of counter;) {
    Execute multiple instructions here
}
```

`for` is a keyword in Solidity and it informs the compiler that it contains information about looping a set of instructions. It is very similar to the `while` loop; however it is more succinct and readable since all information can be viewed in a single line.

The following code example shows the same solution: looping through a mapping. However, it uses the `for` loop instead of the `while` loop. The `i` variable is initialized, incremented by 1 in every iterator, and checked to see whether it is less than the value of `counter`. The loop will stop as soon as the condition becomes false; that is, the value of `i` is equal to or greater than `counter`:

```solidity
pragma solidity ^0.4.19;


contract ForLoopExample {

    mapping (uint => uint) blockNumber;
    uint counter;

    event uintNumber(uint);

    function SetNumber()  {

        blockNumber[counter++] = block.number;

    }

    function getNumbers() {

        for (uint i=0; i < counter; i++){
            uintNumber( blockNumber[i]  );
        }

    }
}
```

The do...while loop

The do...while loop is very similar to the while loop. The general form of a do...while loop is as follows:

```
Declare and Initialize a counter
do {
Execute the instructions here
Increment the value of counter
} while(check the value of counter using an expression or condition)
```

There is a subtle difference between the while and do...while loops. If you notice, the condition in do...while is placed towards the end of the loop instructions. The instructions in the while loop is not executed at all if the condition is false; however, the instruction in the do...while loop get executed once, before the condition is evaluated. So, if you want to execute the instructions at least once, the do...while loop should be preferred compared to the while loop. Take a look at the following screenshot of a code snippet:

```solidity
pragma solidity ^0.4.19;

contract DowhileLoop {

    mapping (uint => uint) blockNumber;
    uint counter;

    event uintNumber(uint);
    bytes aa;

    function SetNumber()  {

        blockNumber[counter++] = block.number;


    }

    function getNumbers() {

        uint i = 0;
        do  {
            uintNumber( blockNumber[i]  );
            i = i + 1;
        } while (i < counter);


    }
}
```

The break statement

Loops help iterateing over from the start till it arives on a vector data type. However, there are times when you would like to stop the iteration in between and jump out or exit from the loop without executing the conditional test again. The break statement helps us do that. It helps us terminate the loop by passing the control to the first instruction after the loop.

In the following screenshot example, the for loop is terminated and control moves out of the for loop when the value of i is 1 because of the use of the break statement. It literally breaks the loop as shown in the following screenshot:

```solidity
pragma solidity ^0.4.19;

contract ForLoopExampleBreak {

    mapping (uint => uint) blockNumber;
    uint counter;

    event uintNumber(uint);

    function SetNumber()  {

        blockNumber[counter++] = block.number;

    }

    function getNumbers() {

        for (uint i=0; i < counter; i++){
            if (i == 1)
                break;
            uintNumber( blockNumber[i]  );

        }

    }
}
```

The continue statement

Loops are based on expressions. The logic of the expression decides the continuity of the loop. However, there are times when you are in between loop execution and would like to go back to the first line of code without executing the rest of the code for the next iteration. The `continue` statement helps us do that.

In the following screenshot, the `for` loop is executed till the end; however the values after 5 are not logged at all:

```solidity
pragma solidity ^0.4.19;

contract ForLoopExampleContinue {

    mapping (uint => uint) blockNumber;
    uint counter;

    event uintNumber(uint);

    function SetNumber()  {

        blockNumber[counter++] = block.number;


    }

    function getNumbers() {

        for (uint i=0; i < counter; i++){
            if ((i > 5) )
                { continue;}
            uintNumber( blockNumber[i]  );

        }

    }
}
```

The return statement

Returning data is an integral part of a Solidity function. Solidity provides two different syntaxes for returning data from a function. In the following code sample, two functions—getBlockNumber and getBlockNumber1—are defined. The getBlockNumber function returns a uint without naming the return variable. In such cases, developers can resort to using the return keyword explicitly to return from the function.

The getBlockNumber1 function returns uint and also provides a name for the variable. In such cases, developers can directly use and return this variable from a function without using the return keyword as shown in the following screenshot:

```solidity
pragma solidity ^0.4.19;

contract ReturnValues {

    uint counter;

    function SetNumber()  {

        counter = block.number;

    }

    function getBlockNumber() returns (uint) {

        return counter;

    }

    function getBlockNumber1() returns (uint result) {

        result =  counter;

    }
}
```

Summary

Expressions and control structures are an integral part of any programming language and they are an important element of the Solidity language as well. Solidity provides a rich infrastructure for decision and looping constructs. It provides if...else decision control structures and the for, do...while, and while loops for looping over data variables that can be iterated. Solidity also allows us to write conditions and logical, assignment, and other types of statement any that programming language supports.

The following chapter will discuss Solidity and contract functions in detail; these are core elements for writing contracts. Blockchain is about executing and storing transactions and transactions are created when contract functions are executed. Functions can change the state of Ethereum or just return the current state. Functions that change state and those that return—current state will be discussed in detail in the following chapter.

6
Writing Smart Contracts

Solidity is used to author smart contracts. This chapter is dedicated to smart contracts. It is from here that you will start writing smart contracts. This chapter will discuss the design aspects of writing smart contracts, defining and implementing a contract, and deploying and creating contracts using different mechanisms—using new keywords and known addresses. Solidity provides rich object orientation and this chapter will delve deep into object-oriented concepts and implementations, such as inheritance, multiple inheritance, declaring abstract classes and interfaces, and providing method implementations to abstract functions and interfaces.

This chapter covers the following topics:

- Creating contracts
- Creating contracts via `new`
- Inheritance
- Abstract contracts
- Interfaces

Smart contracts

What are smart contracts? Everybody bears an expression trying to understand the meaning of contracts and the significance of the word "smart" in reference to contracts. Smart contracts are, essentially, code segments or programs that are deployed and executed in EVM. A contract is a term generally used in the legal world and has little relevance in the programming world. Writing a smart contract in Solidity does not mean writing a legal contract. Moreover, contracts are like any other programming code, containing Solidity code, and are executed when someone invokes them. There is inherently nothing smart about it. A smart contract is a blockchain term; it is a piece of jargon used to refer to programming logic and code that executes within EVM.

A smart contract is very similar to a C++, Java, or C# class. Just as a class is composed of state (variables) and behaviors (methods), contracts contain state variables and functions. The purpose of state variables is to maintain the current state of the contract, and functions are responsible for executing logic and performing update and read operations on the current state.

We have already seen some examples of smart contracts in the previous chapter; however, it's time to dive deeper into the subject.

Writing a simple contract

A contract is declared using the `contract` keyword along with an identifier, as shown in the following code snippet:

```
contract SampleContract {
}
```

Within the brackets comes the declaration of state variables and function definitions. A complete definition of contract was discussed in `Chapter 3`, *Introducing Solidity*, and I am providing it again for quick reference. This contract has state variables, struct definitions, enum declarations, function definitions, modifiers, and events. State variables, structs, and enums were discussed in detail in `Chapter 4`, *Global Variables and Functions*. Functions, modifiers, and events will be discussed in detail over the next two chapters. Take a look at the following screenshot of a code snippet depicting contract:

```
pragma solidity 0.4.19;

//contract definition
contract generalStructure {
    //state variables
    int public stateIntVariable; // vriable of integer type
    string stateStringVariable; //variable of string type
    address personIdentifier; // variable of address type
    myStruct human; // variable of structure type
    bool constant hasIncome = true; //variable of constant nature

    //structure definition
    struct myStruct {
        string name; //variable fo type string
        uint myAge; // variable of unsigned integer type
        bool isMarried; // variable of boolean type
        uint[] bankAccountsNumbers; // variable - dynamic array of unsigned integer
    }

    //modifier declaration
    modifier onlyBy(){
        if (msg.sender == personIdentifier) {
            _;
        }
    }

    // event declaration
    event ageRead(address, int );

    //enumeration declaration
    enum gender {male, female}

    //function definition
    function getAge (address _personIdentifier) onlyBy() payable external returns (uint) {

        human =  myStruct("Ritesh",10,true,new uint[](3)); //using struct myStruct

        gender _gender = gender.male; //using enum

        ageRead(personIdentifier, stateIntVariable);
    }
}
```

Creating contracts

There are the following two ways of creating and using a contract in Solidity:

- Using the new keyword
- Using the address of the already deployed contract

Using the new keyword

The new keyword in Solidity deploys and creates a new contract instance. It initializes the contract instance by deploying the contract, initializing the state variables, running its constructor, setting the nonce value to one, and, eventually, returns the address of the instance to the caller. Deploying a contract involves checking whether the requestor has provided enough gas to complete deployment, generating a new account/address for contract deployment using the requestor's address and nonce value, and passing on any Ether sent along with it.

In the next screenshot, two contracts, HelloWorld and client, are defined. In this scenario, one contract (client) deploys and creates a new instance of another contract (HelloWorld). It does so using the new keyword as shown in the following code snippet:

```
HelloWorld myObj = new HelloWorld();
```

Let's take a look at the following screenshot:

```solidity
pragma solidity 0.4.19;

contract HelloWorld {
    uint private simpleInt;

    function  getValue() public view returns (uint) {
        return simpleInt;
    }

    function setValue(uint _value) public {
        simpleInt = _value;
    }
}


contract client  {

    function useNewKeyword() public  returns (uint) {

        HelloWorld myObj = new HelloWorld();

        myObj.setValue(10);

        return myObj.getValue();

    }
}
```

Using address of a contract

This method of creating a contract instance is used when a contract is already deployed and instantiated. This method of creating a contract uses the address of an existing, deployed contract. No new instance is created; rather, an existing instance is reused. A reference to the existing contract is made using its address.

In the next code illustration, two contracts, HelloWorld and client, are defined. In this scenario, one contract(client) uses an already known address of another contract to create a reference to it (HelloWorld). It does so using the address data type and casting the actual address to the HelloWorld contract type. The myObj object contains the address of an existing contract, as shown in the following code snippet:

```
HelloWorld myObj = HelloWorld(obj);
```

Let's take a look at the following screenshot:

```solidity
pragma solidity 0.4.19;

contract HelloWorld {

    uint private simpleInt;

    function  GetValue() public view returns (uint) {
        return simpleInt;
    }

    function  SetValue(uint _value) public {
        simpleInt = _value;
    }
}


contract client  {

    address obj ;

    function setObject(address _obj) external   {
        obj = _obj;
    }

    function UseExistingAddress() public  returns (uint) {
        HelloWorld myObj = HelloWorld(obj);
        myObj.SetValue(10);
        return myObj.GetValue();
    }
}
```

Constructors

Solidity supports declaring a constructor within a contract. Constructors are optional in Solidity and the compiler induces a default constructor when no constructor is explicitly defined. The constructor is executed once while deploying the contract. This is quite different from other programming languages. In other programming languages, a constructor is executed whenever a new object instance is created. However, in Solidity, a constructor is executed are deployed on EVM. Constructors should be used for initializing state variables and, generally, writing extensive Solidity code should be avoided. The constructor code is the first set of code that is executed for a contract. There can be at most one constructor in a contract, unlike constructors in other programming languages. Constructors can take parameters and arguments should be supplied while deploying the contract.

A constructor has the same name as that of the contract. Both the names should be the same. A constructor can be either `public` or `internal`, from a visibility point of view. It cannot be `external` or `private`. A constructor does not return any data explicitly. In the following example, a constructor with the same name as that of the `HelloWorld` contract is defined. It sets the storage variable value to 5, as shown in the following screenshot:

```solidity
pragma solidity 0.4.19;

contract HelloWorld {

    uint private simpleInt;

    function HelloWorld() public {
        simpleInt = 5;
    }

    function  GetValue() public view returns (uint) {
        return simpleInt;
    }

    function  SetValue(uint _value) public {
        simpleInt = _value;
    }
}
```

Contract composition

Solidity supports contract composition. Composition refers to combining multiple contracts or data types together to create complex data structures and contracts. We have already seen numerous examples of contract composition before. Refer to the code snippet for creating contracts using the `new` keyword shown earlier in this chapter. In this example, the `client` contract is composed of the `HelloWorld` contract. Here, `HelloWorld` is an independent contract and `client` is a dependent contract. `client` is a dependent contract because it is dependent on the `HelloWorld` contract for its completeness. It is a good practice to break down problems into multi-contract solutions and compose them together using contract composition.

Inheritance

Inheritance is one of the pillars of object orientation and Solidity supports inheritance between smart contracts. Inheritance is the process of defining multiple contracts that are related to each other through parent-child relationships. The contract that is inherited is called the **parent contract** and the contract that inherits is called the **child contract**. Similarly, the contract has a parent known as the **derived class** and the parent contract is known as a **base contract**. Inheritance is mostly about code-reusability. There is a is-a relationship between base and derived contracts and all public and internal scoped functions and state variables are available to derived contracts. In fact, Solidity compiler copies the base contract bytecode into derived contract bytecode. The `is` keyword is used to inherit the base contract in the derived contract.

It is one of the most important concepts that should be mastered by every Solidity developer because of the way contracts are versioned and deployed.

Solidity supports multiple types of inheritance, including multiple inheritance.

Solidity copies the base contracts into the derived contract and a single contract is created with inheritance. A single address is generated that is shared between contracts in a parent-child relationship.

Single inheritance

Single inheritance helps in inheriting the variables, functions, modifiers, and events of base contracts into the derived class. Take a look at the following diagram:

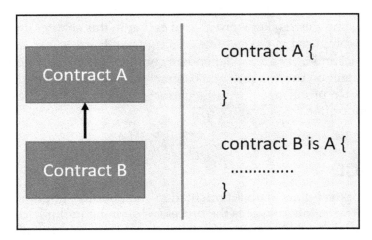

The next code snippets help to explain single inheritance. You will observe that there are two contracts, ParentContract and ChildContract. The ChildContract contract inherits from ParentContract. ChildContract will inherit all public and internal variables and functions. Anybody using ChildContract, as seen in the client contract, can invoke both GetInteger and SetInteger functions as if they were defined in ChildContract, as shown in the following screenshot:

```
pragma solidity 0.4.19;

contract ParentContract {
    uint internal simpleInteger;

    function SetInteger(uint _value) external {
        simpleInteger = _value;
    }
}


contract ChildContract is ParentContract  {
    bool private simpleBool;

    function  GetInteger() public view returns (uint) {
        return simpleInteger;
    }
}



contract Client  {
    ChildContract pc = new ChildContract();

    function workWithInheritance() public  returns (uint) {
        pc.SetInteger(100);
        return pc.GetInteger();
    }
}
```

All functions in Solidity contracts are virtual and are based on contract instance. An appropriate function—either in the base or derived class is invoked. This topic is known as **polymorphism** and is covered in a later section in this chapter.

The order of invocation of the contract constructor is from the base most contract to the derive most contract.

Multi-level inheritance

Multi-level inheritance is very similar to single inheritance; however, instead of just a single parent-child relationship, there are multiple levels of parent-child relationship.

This is shown in the following diagram. **Contract A** is the parent of **Contract B** and **Contract B** is the parent of **Contract C**:

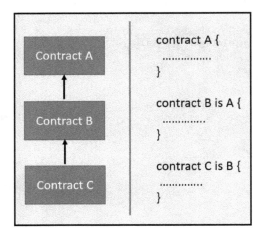

Hierarchical inheritance

Hierarchical inheritance is again similar to simple inheritance. Here, however, a single contract acts as a base contract for multiple derived contracts. This is shown in the following diagram. Here, **Contract A** is derived in both **Contract B** and **Contract C**:

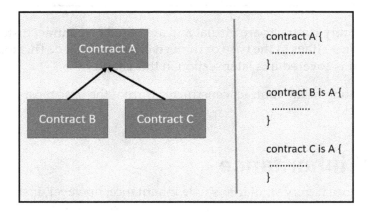

Multiple inheritance

Solidity supports multiple inheritance. There can be multiple levels of single inheritance. However, there can also be multiple contracts that derive from the same base contract. These derived contracts can be used as base contracts together in further child classes. When contracts inherit from such child contracts together, there is multiple inheritance, as shown in the following diagram:

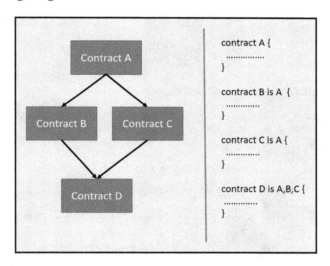

The next screenshot shows an example of multiple inheritance. In this example, SumContract acts as a base contract that is derived into the MultiContract and DivideContract contracts. The SumContract contract provides an implementation for the Sum function and the MultiContract and DivideContract contracts provide an implementation of the Multiply and Divide functions, respectively. Both MultiContract and DivideContract are inherited in SubContract. The SubContract contract provides an implementation of the Sub function. The client contract is not a part of the parent-child hierarchy and is consuming other contracts. The client contract creates an instance of SubContract and calls the Sum method on it.

Solidity follows the path of Python and uses **C3 Linearization**, also known as **Method Resolution Order (MRO)**, to force a specific order in graphs of base contracts. The contracts should follow a specific order while inheriting, starting from the base contract through to the most derived contract. An example of such sequencing is shown next, in which the SubContract contract is derived from SumContract, DivideContract, and MultiContract.

The following screenshot of the code example shows that `MultiContract` is an immediate parent contract for the `SubContract` contract, followed by `DivideContract` and `SumContract`:

```solidity
pragma solidity 0.4.19;

contract SumContract {

    function Sum(uint a, uint b) public returns (uint) {
        return  a + b;
    }

}

contract MultiContract is SumContract  {

    function Multiply(uint a, uint b) public returns (uint) {
        return  a * b;
    }

}

contract DivideContract is SumContract  {

    function Divide(uint a, uint b) public returns (uint) {
        return  a / b;
    }
}

contract SubContract is SumContract, MultiContract,DivideContract

    function sub(uint a, uint b) public returns (uint) {
        return  a - b;
    }
}

contract client  {

    function workWithInheritance() public  returns (uint) {
        uint a = 20;
        uint b = 10;
        SubContract subt = new SubContract();
        return subt.Sum(a,b);
    }
}
```

It is also possible to invoke a function specific to a contract by using the contract name along with the function name.

Encapsulation

Encapsulation is one of the most important pillars of OOP. Encapsulation refers to the process of hiding or allowing access to state variables directly for changing their state. It refers to the pattern of declaring variables that cannot be accessed directly by clients and can only be modified using functions. This helps in constraint access to variables but, at the same time, allows enough access to class for taking action on it. Solidity provides multiple visibility modifiers such as `external`, `public`, `internal`, and `private` that affects the visibility of state variables within the contract in which they are defined, inheriting child contracts or outside contracts.

Polymorphism

Polymorphism means having multiple forms. There are the following two types of polymorphism:

- Function polymorphism
- Contract polymorphism

Function polymorphism

Function polymorphism refers to declaring multiple functions within the same contract or inheriting contracts having the same name. The functions differ in the parameter data types or in the number of parameters. Return types are not taken into consideration for determining valid function signatures for polymorphism. This is also known as **method overloading**.

The next code segment illustrates a contract that contains two functions, which have the same name but different data types for incoming parameters. The first function, getVariableData, accepts int8 as its parameter data type, while the next function having the same name accepts int16 as its parameter data type. It is absolutely legal to have the same function name with a different number of parameters of different data types for incoming parameters as shown in the following screenshot:

```solidity
pragma solidity ^0.4.19;

contract HelloFunctionPolymorphism
{
    function getVariableData(int8 data) public constant returns(int8 output)
    {
        return data;
    }

    function overloadedFunction(int16 data) public constant returns(int16 output)
    {
        return data;
    }
}
```

Contract polymorphism

Contract polymorphism refers to using multiple contract instances interchangeably when the contracts are related to each other by way of inheritance. Contract polymorphism helps in invoking derived contract functions using a base contract instance.

Let's understand this concept with the help of code listing shown next.

A parent contract contains two functions, SetInteger and GetInteger. A child contract inherits from a parent contract and provides its own implementation of GetInteger. The child contract can be created using the ChildContract variable data type and it can also be created using the parent contract data type. Polymorphism allows the use of any contract in a parent-child relationship with the base type contract variable. The contract instance decides which function will be invoked—the base or derived contract.

Take a look at the following code snippet:

```
ParentContract pc = new ChildContract();
```

The preceding code creates a child contract and stores the reference in the parent contract type variable. This is how contract polymorphism is implemented in Solidity as shown in the following screenshot:

```solidity
pragma solidity ^0.4.19;

contract ParentContract {

    uint internal simpleInteger;

    function SetInteger(uint _value) public {
        simpleInteger = _value;
    }

    function GetInteger() public view returns (uint) {
        return 10;
    }
}

contract ChildContract is ParentContract  {

    function GetInteger() public view returns (uint) {
        return simpleInteger;
    }
}

contract client  {

    ParentContract pc = new ChildContract();

    function workWithInheritance() public returns (uint) {
        pc.SetInteger(100);
        return pc.GetInteger();
    }
}
```

Method overriding

Method overriding refers to redefining a function available in the parent contract having the same name and signature in the derived contract. The next code segment shows this. A parent contract contains two functions, SetInteger and GetInteger. A child contract inherits from the parent contract and provides its own implementation of GetInteger by overriding the function.

Now, when a call to the `GetInteger` function is made on the child contract even while using a parent contract variable, the child contract instance function is invoked. This is because all functions in contracts are virtual and based on contract instance; the most derived function is invoked, as shown in the following screenshot:

```solidity
pragma solidity ^0.4.19;

contract ParentContract {

    uint internal simpleInteger;

    function SetInteger(uint _value) public {
        simpleInteger = _value;
    }

    function GetInteger() public view returns (uint) {
        return 10;
    }
}

contract ChildContract is ParentContract  {

    function GetInteger() public view returns (uint) {
        return simpleInteger;
    }
}

contract client  {

    ParentContract pc = new ChildContract();

    function workWithInheritance() public returns (uint) {
        pc.SetInteger(100);
        return pc.GetInteger();
    }
}
```

Abstract contracts

Abstracts contracts are contracts that have partial function definitions. You cannot create an instance of an abstract contract. An abstract contract must be inherited by a child contract for utilizing its functions. Abstract contracts help in defining the structure of a contract and any class inheriting from it must ensure to provide an implementation for them. If the child contract does not provide the implementation for incomplete functions, even its instance cannot be created. The function signatures terminate using the semicolon, `;`, character. There is no Solidity-provided keyword to mark a contract as abstract. A contract becomes an abstract class if it has functions without implementation.

The screenshot shown next is an implementation of an abstract contract. The abstractHelloWorld contract is an abstract contract as it contains a couple of functions without any definitions. GetValue and SetValue are function signatures without any implementation. There is another method that returns a constant. The purpose of AddaNumber is to show that there can be functions within an abstract contract containing implementation as well. The abstractHelloWorld abstract contract is inherited by the HelloWorld contract that provides implementation for all the methods. The client contract creates an instance of the HelloWorld contract using the base contract variable and invokes its functions as shown in the following screenshot:

```solidity
pragma solidity 0.4.19;

contract abstractHelloWorld {
    function  GetValue() public view returns (uint);
    function  SetValue(uint _value) public;

    function AddaNumber(uint _value) public returns (uint){
        return 10;
    }

}


contract HelloWorld is abstractHelloWorld{
    uint private simpleInteger;

    function  GetValue() public view returns (uint) {
        return simpleInteger;
    }

    function  SetValue(uint _value) public {
        simpleInteger = _value;

    }

    function AddaNumber(uint _value) public returns (uint){
        return simpleInteger + _value;
    }
}


contract client  {

    abstractHelloWorld myObj ;

    function client(){
        myObj = new HelloWorld();
    }

    function  GetSetIntegerValue() public  returns (uint) {
        myObj.SetValue(100);
        return  myObj.AddaNumber(200);
    }

}
```

Interfaces

Interfaces are like abstract contracts, but there are differences. Interfaces cannot contain any definition. They can only contain function declarations. It means functions in interfaces cannot contain any code. They are also known as **pure** abstract contracts. An interface can contain only the signature of functions. It also cannot contain any state variables. They cannot inherit from other contracts or contain enums or structures. However, interfaces can inherit other interfaces. The function signatures terminate using the semicolon ; character. Interfaces are declared using the interface keyword following by an identifier. The next code example shows an implementation of the interface. Solidity provides the interface keyword for declaring interfaces. The IHelloWorld interface is defined containing two function signatures—GetValue and SetValue. There are no functions containing any implementation. IHelloWorld is implemented by the HelloWorld contract. Contract intent to use this contract would create an instance as it would do normally as shown in the following screenshot:

```
pragma solidity 0.4.19;

interface IHelloWorld {
    function  GetValue() public view returns (uint);
    function  SetValue(uint _value) public;
}


contract HelloWorld is IHelloWorld{
    uint private simpleInteger;

    function  GetValue() public view returns (uint) {
        return simpleInteger;
    }

    function  SetValue(uint _value) public {
        simpleInteger = _value;

    }
}


contract client  {

    IHelloWorld myObj ;

    function client(){
        myObj = new HelloWorld();
    }

    function  GetSetIntegerValue() public  returns (uint) {
        myObj.SetValue(100);
        return  myObj.GetValue();
    }

}
```

Summary

This brings us to the end of this chapter. It was a heavy chapter that focused primarily on smart contracts, the different ways to create an instance, and all the important object-oriented concepts related to them, including inheritance, polymorphism, abstraction, and encapsulation. Multiple types of inheritance can be implemented in Solidity. Simple, multiple, hierarchical, and multi-level inheritance were discussed, along with usage and implementation of abstract contracts and interfaces. It should be noted that using inheritance in Solidity, there is eventually just one contract that is deployed instead of multiple contracts. There is just one address that can be used by any contract with a parent-child hierarchy.

The next chapter will focus purely on functions within contracts. Functions are central to writing effective Solidity contracts. These are functions that help change the contract state and retrieve them. Without functions, having any meaningful smart contracts is difficult. Functions have different visibility scope, multiple attributes are available that affect their behavior, and also help in accepting Ether. Stay tuned for a function ride in the next chapter!

7
Functions, Modifiers, and Fallbacks

Solidity is maturing and providing advanced programming constructs so that users can write better smart contracts. This chapter is dedicated to some of the most important smart contract constructs, such as functions, modifiers, and fallbacks. Functions are the most important element of a smart contract after state variables. It is functions that help to create transactions and implement custom logic in Ethereum. There are various types of functions, which will be discussed in depth in this chapter. Modifiers are special functions that help in writing more readily available and modular smart contracts. Fallbacks are a concept unique to contract-based programming languages, and they are executed when a function call does not match any existing declared method in the contract. Finally, every function has visibility attached to it that affects its availability to the external caller, other contracts, and contracts in inheritance.

This chapter covers the following topics:

- Input parameters and output parameters
- Returning multiple parameters
- View functions
- Pure functions
- Scopes and declarations
- Visibility and getters
- Internal function calls

- External function calls
- Modifiers
- Fallback functions

Function input and output

Functions would not be that interesting if they didn't accept parameters and return values. Functions are made generic with the use of parameters and return values. Parameters can help in changing function execution and providing different execution paths. Solidity allows you to accept multiple parameters within the same function; the only condition is that their identifiers should be uniquely named.

The following code snippets show the following multiple functions, each with different constructs for parameters and return values:

1. The first function, `singleIncomingParameter`, accepts one parameter named `_data` of type `int` and returns a single return value that is identified using `_output` of type `int`. The `function` signature provides constructs to define both the incoming parameters and return values. The `return` keyword in the `function` signature helps define the return types from the function. In the following code snippet, the `return` keyword within the function code automatically maps to the first `return` type declared in the `function` signature:

```
function singleIncomingParameter(int _data) returns (int
_output) {
    return _data * 2;
}
```

2. The second function, `multipleIncomingParameter`, accepts two parameters: `_data` and `_data2`, which are both of type `int` and return a single return value identified using `_output` of type `int`, as follows:

```
function multipleIncomingParameter(int _data, int _data2)
returns (int _output) {
    return _data * _data2;
}
```

3. The third function, `multipleOutgoingParameter`, accepts one parameter, `_data`, of type `int` and returns two return values identified using `square` and `half`, which are both of type `int`. In the following code snippet, returning multiple parameters is something unique to Solidity and is not found in many programming languages:

```
function multipleOutgoingParameter(int _data) returns (int
square, int half)
{
    square = _data * _data;
    half = _data /2 ;
}
```

4. The fourth function, `multipleOutgoingTuple`, is similar to the third function mentioned previously. However, instead of assigning return values as separate statements and variables, it returns values as a tuple. A **tuple** is a custom data structure consisting of multiple variables, as shown in the following code snippet:

```
function multipleOutgoingTuple(int _data) returns (int square,
int half)
{
    (square, half) = (_data * _data,_data /2 );
}
```

The entire contract code is shown in the following screenshot:

```
pragma solidity ^0.4.19;

contract Parameters {

    function singleIncomingParameter(int _data) returns (int _output) {
        return _data * 2;
    }

    function multipleIncomingParameter(int _data, int _data2) returns (int _output) {
        return _data * _data2;
    }

    function multipleOutgoingParameter(int _data) returns (int square, int half) {
        square = _data * _data;
        half = _data /2 ;
    }

    function multipleOutgoingTuple(int _data) returns (int square, int half) {
        (square, half) = (_data * _data,_data /2 );
    }
}
```

It is also possible to declare parameters without any identifier at all. This feature does not have much utility, however, as those parameters cannot be referenced within the function code. Similarly, return values can be declared without any name.

Modifiers

Modifiers are another concept unique to Solidity. Modifiers help in modifying the behavior of a function. Let's try to understand this with the help of an example. The following code does not use modifiers; in this contract, two state variables, two functions, and a constructor are defined. One of the state variables stores the address of the account deploying the contract. Within the constructor, the global variable msg.sender is used to input the account value in the owner state variable. The two functions check whether the caller is the same as the account that deployed the contract; if it is, the function code is executed, otherwise it ignores the rest of the code. While this code works as is, it can be made better both in terms of readability and manageability. This is where modifiers can help. In this example, the checks are made using the if conditional statements. Later, in the next chapter, we will see how to use new Solidity constructs, such as require and assert, to execute the same checks without if conditions. Take a look at the following screenshot of the code snippet depicting modifiers:

```solidity
pragma solidity ^0.4.17;

contract ContractWithoutModifier {

    address owner;
    int public mydata;

    function ContractWithoutModifier(){
        owner = msg.sender;
    }

    function AssignDoubleValue(int _data) public  {
        if(msg.sender == owner) {
            mydata = _data * 2;
        }
    }

    function AssignTenerValue(int _data) public  {
        if(msg.sender == owner) {
            mydata = _data * 10;
        }
    }

}
```

Modifiers are special functions that change the behavior of a function. Here, the function code remains the same, but the execution path of a function changes. Modifiers can only be applied to functions. Let's now see how to write the same contract using modifiers shown in the following screenshot:

```solidity
pragma solidity ^0.4.17;


contract ContractWithModifier {

    address owner;
    int public mydata;

    function ContractWithoutModifier(){
        owner = msg.sender;
    }

    modifier isOwner {
        // require(msg.sender == owner);
        if(msg.sender == owner) {
            _;
        }
    }

    function AssignDoubleValue(int _data) public isOwner {
            mydata = _data * 2;
    }

    function AssignTenerValue(int _data) public  {
            mydata = _data * 10;
    }

}
```

The contract shown here has the same constructs: a constructor, two state variables, and two functions. It also has an additional special function that is defined using the `modifier` keyword. The function code for both the `AssignDoubleValue` and `AssignTenerValue` functions are different, although they have similar functionality. These functions do not use the `if` condition to check whether the caller of the function is the same as the account that deployed the contract; instead, these functions are decorated with the modifier name in their signature.

Let's now try to understand the modifier construct in Solidity and its usage.

Modifiers are defined using the `modifier` keyword and an identifier. The code for modifier is placed within curly brackets. The code within a modifier can validate the incoming value and can conditionally execute the called function after evaluation. The _ identifier is of special importance here—its purpose is to replace itself with the function code that is invoked by the caller.

When a caller calls the `AssignDoubleValue` function, which is decorated with the `isOwner` modifier, the modifier takes control of the execution and replaces the _ identifier with the called function code, that is, `AssignDoubleValue`. Eventually, in EVM, the modifier looks like the following code during runtime:

```
modifier isOwner {
// require(msg.sender == owner);
if(msg.sender == owner) {
mydata = _data * 2;
}
}
```

The same modifier can be applied to multiple functions, and the _ identifier can be replaced to the called function code.

This helps in writing cleaner, more readable, and more maintainable code. Developers do not have to keep repeating the same code in every function or check for the incoming value when executing a function.

The view, constant, and pure functions

Solidity provides special modifiers for functions, such as `view`, `pure`, and `constant`. These are also known as **state mutability** attributes because they define the scope of changes allowed within the Ethereum global state. The purpose of these modifiers is similar to those discussed previously, but there are some small differences. This section will detail the use of these keywords.

Writing smart contract functions helps primarily with the following three activities:

- Updating state variables
- Reading state variables
- Logic execution

The execution of functions and transactions costs gas and is not free of cost. Every transaction needs a specified amount of gas based on its execution and callers are responsible for supplying that gas for successful execution. This is true for transactions or for any activity that modifies the global state of Ethereum.

There are functions that are only responsible for reading and returning the state variable, and these are like property getters in other programming languages. They read the current value in a state variable and return values back to the caller. These functions do not change the state of Ethereum. Ethereum's documentation (http://solidity.readthedocs.io/en/ v0.4.21/contracts.html) mentions the following statements in relation to things that modify state:

- Writing to state variables
- Emitting events
- Creating other contracts
- Using `selfdestruct`
- Sending Ether via calls
- Calling any function not marked `view` or `pure`
- Using low-level calls
- Using inline assembly that contains certain opcodes

Solidity developers can mark their functions with the `view` modifier to suggest to EVM that this function does not change the Ethereum state or any activity mentioned before. Currently, this is not enforced, but it is expected to be in the future.

An example of the `view` function is shown in the following screenshot:

```
pragma solidity ^0.4.17;

contract ViewFunction {

    function GetTenerValue(int _data) public view returns (int)  {
            return _data * 10;
    }

}
```

If you have functions that just return values without any modification of state, they can be marked with the `view` function.

It is also worth noting that the `view` functions are also known as **constant** functions. The `constant` functions were used in previous versions of Solidity.

The `pure` functions are more restrictive in terms of state mutability when compared to the `view` functions; however, their purpose is the same, that is, to restrict state mutability. It is also worth noting that even the `pure` functions are not enforced as of the time of writing, but we expect it to be in the future.

The `pure` functions add further restrictions on top of the `view` functions; for example, a `pure` function is not allowed to even read the current state of Ethereum. In short, the `pure` functions disallow reading and writing to Ethereum's global state. The additional activities not allowed according to documentation include the following:

- Reading from state variables
- Accessing `this.balance` or `<address>.balance`
- Accessing any of the members of `block`, `tx`, and `msg` (with the exception of `msg.sig` and `msg.data`)
- Calling any function not marked `pure`
- Using inline assembly that contains certain opcodes

The previous function has been rewritten as a `pure` function in the following screenshot:

```solidity
pragma solidity ^0.4.17;


contract PureFunction {

    function GetTenerValue(int _data) public pure returns (int)  {
            return _data * 10;
    }

}
```

The address functions

In the chapter relating to data types, we purposely did not explain the functions related to the `address` data type. Although these functions could have been covered there, some of these functions can execute a fallback function automatically, and hence it is covered here.

Address provides five functions and a single property.

The only property provided by `address` is the `balance` property, which provides the balance available in an account (contract or individual) in wei, as shown in the following code snippet:

```
<<account>>.balance ;
```

In the preceding code, `account` is a valid Ethereum address and this returns the balance available in this in terms of wei.

Now, let's take a look at the methods provided by an account.

The send method

The `send` method is used to send Ether to a contract or to an individually owned account. Take a look at the following code depicting the `send` method:

```
<<account>>.send(amount);
```

The `send` function provides 2,300 gas as a fixed limit, which cannot be superseded. This is especially important when sending an amount to a contract address. To send an amount to an individually owned account, this amount of gas is enough. The `send` function returns a boolean `true`/`false` as a return value. In this case, an exception is not returned; instead, `false` is returned from the function. If everything goes right in an execution, `true` is returned from the function. If `send` is used along with the contract address, it will invoke the fallback function on the contract. We will investigate fallback functions in detail in the following section.

Now, let's see an example of the `send` function, as shown in the following screenshot:

```
function SimpleSendToAccount() public returns (bool) {
    return msg.sender.send(1);
}
```

In the preceding screenshot, the `send` function sent 1 wei to the caller of the `SimpleSendToAccount` function. We already learned about `msg.sender` in previous chapters dealing with global variables.

`send` is a low-level function and should be used with caution as it can invoke fallback functions that may recursively call back within the calling contract again and again. There is a pattern known as **Check-Deduct-Transfer (CDF)**, or sometimes as **Check-Effects-Interaction (CEI)**, which we look at in the following screenshot. In this pattern, it is assumed that balances are maintained within a mapping. The `mapping` consists of an address and its associated balance, as shown in the following screenshot:

```
mapping (address => uint) balance;

function SimpleSendToAccount(uint amount) public returns (bool) {
    if(balance[msg.sender] >= amount ) {
        balance[msg.sender] -= amount;
        if (msg.sender.send(amount) == true) {
            return true;
        }
        else {
            balance[msg.sender] += amount;
            return false;
        }
    }
}
```

In this example, a check is first made to see if the caller has a sufficient balance to withdraw funds. If it has, we can reduce the amount from the existing balance and call the `send` method. Then, we must check that `send` is successful; if not, return the amount.

It is worth noting that a lot of sources claim `send` is being deprecated, but I do not think it is. There are specific usages of the `send` function still available, such as sending an amount to multiple accounts. However, a new function transfer has been introduced to send Ether from one account to another; an even better solution would be to ask other contracts and accounts to call a specific method to withdraw the amount.

The transfer method

The `transfer` method is similar to the `send` method. It is responsible for sending Ether or wei to an address. However, the difference here is that `transfer` raises an exception in the case of execution failure, instead of returning `false`, and all changes are reverted. Take a look at the `transfer` method in the following screenshot:

```
function SimpleTransferToAccount() public  {
    msg.sender.transfer(1);
}
```

The `transfer` method is preferred over the `send` method as it raises an exception in the event of an error, meaning exceptions are bubbled up in the stack and halt execution.

The call method

The `call` method has resulted in a lot of confusion among developers. There is a `call` method available via the `web3.eth` object, and there is also the `<<address>>.call` function. These are two different functions that have different purposes.

The `web3.eth` call method can only make calls to a node it is connected to and is a read-only operation. It is not allowed to change the state of Ethereum. It does not generate a transaction nor does it consume any gas. It is used to call the `pure`, `constant`, and `view` functions.

On the other hand, call function provided by address data type can call any function available within a contract. There are times when the interface of contract, more commonly known as ABI, is not available, and so the only way to invoke a function is to use the `call` method. This method does not adhere to ABI and can call any function on a need-to-know basis. There is no compile time check available for these calls, and they return a boolean value of either `true` or `false`.

It is worth noting that it is not an ideal practice to call a `contract` function using the `call` method, as there are no checks and validation involved.

Every function in a contract is identified at runtime using a 4-bytes identifier. This 4-bytes identifier is the trimmed-down hash of a function name along with its parameter types. After hashing the function name and parameter types, the first four bytes are considered as the function identifier. The `call` function accepts these bytes to call the function as the first parameter and the actual parameter values as subsequent parameters.

A `call` function without any function parameter is shown in the following code. Here, `SetBalance` does not take any parameter:

```
myaddr.call(bytes4(sha3("SetBalance()")));
```

A `call` function with a function parameter is shown in the following snippet. Here, `SetBalance` takes a single `uint` parameter:

```
myaddr.call(bytes4(sha3("SetBalance(uint256)")), 10);
```

It is also worth noting that the `send` function seen previously actually calls the `call` function internally by supplying zero gas to the function.

The following code example shows all the possible ways of using this function. In this example, a contract named `EtherBox` is created with the following two simple functions:

- `SetBalance`: It has a single state variable, and the purpose of this function is to add `10` in every invocation to the existing value of the state variable
- `GetBalance`: This function is responsible for returning the current value of a state variable

Another contract named `usingCall` is created to invoke methods on the `EtherBox` contract via the `call` function. Let's take a look at the following functions mentioned in the upcoming code example:

1. `SimpleCall`: This function creates an instance of the `EtherBox` contract and converts it into an address. Using this address, the `call` function is used to invoke the `SetBalance` function on the `EtherBox` contract.
2. `SimpleCallWithGas`: This function creates an instance of the `EtherBox` contract and converts it into an address. Using this address, the `call` function is used to invoke the `SetBalance` function on `EtherBox`. Alongside the call, gas is also sent along, such that function execution can be completed if it needs more gas.
3. `SimpleCallWithGasAndValue`: This function creates an instance of the `EtherBox` contract and converts it into an address. Using this address, the `call` function is used to invoke the `SetBalance` function on `EtherBox`. Alongside the call, gas is also sent along, such that function execution can be completed if it needs more gas. Apart from gas, it is also possible to send Ether or wei to payable functions.

Take a look at the preceding functions in the following screenshot:

```solidity
pragma solidity ^0.4.17;

contract EtherBox {
    uint balance;

    function SetBalance() public {
        balance = balance + 10;
    }

    function GetBalance() public payable returns(uint) {
        return balance;
    }
}

contract UsingCall {
    function UsingCall() public payable  {
    }

    function SimpleCall() public returns (uint) {
        bool status = true;
        EtherBox eb = new EtherBox();
        address myaddr = address(eb);
        status =   myaddr.call(bytes4(sha3("SetBalance()")));
        return eb.GetBalance();
    }

    function SimpleCallwithGas() public returns (bool) {
        bool status = true;
        EtherBox eb = new EtherBox();
        address myaddr = address(eb);
        status =   myaddr.call.gas(200000)(bytes4(sha3("GetBalance()")));
        return status;
    }

    function SimpleCallwithGasAndValue() public returns (bool) {
        bool status = true;
        EtherBox eb = new EtherBox();
        address myaddr = address(eb);
        status =   myaddr.call.gas(200000).value(1)(bytes4(sha3("GetBalance()")));
        return status;
    }

}
```

The callcode method

This function is deprecated and will not be discussed here. More information about `callcode` is available at `http://solidity.readthedocs.io/en/develop/introduction-to-smart-contracts.html`.

The delegatecall method

This function is, again, a low-level function responsible for calling functions in another contract using the callers's state variables. Generally, it is used along with libraries in Solidity. More information about `delegatecall` is available at: `http://solidity.readthedocs.io/en/develop/introduction-to-smart-contracts.html`.

The fallback function

The fallback functions are a special type of function available only in Ethereum. Solidity helps in writing fallback functions. Imagine a situation where you, as a Solidity developer, are consuming a smart contract by invoking its functions. It is quite possible that you use a function name that does not exist within that contract. In such cases, the fallback function, as the name suggests, would automatically be invoked.

A fallback function is invoked when no function name matches the called function.

A fallback function does not have an identifier or function name. It is defined without a name. Since it cannot be called explicitly, it cannot accept any arguments or return any value. An example of a fallback function is as follows:

```solidity
pragma solidity ^0.4.17;


contract FallbackFunction {

    function () {
        var a = 0;
    }

}
```

A fallback function can also be invoked when a contract receives any Ether. This usually happens using the SendTransaction function available in web3 to send Ether from one account to a contract. However, in this case, the fallback function should be payable, otherwise it will not be able to accept the Ether and will raise an error.

The next important question to be answered is how much gas is needed to execute this function. Since it cannot be called explicitly, gas cannot be sent to this function. Instead, EVM provides a fixed stipend of 2,300 gas to this function. Any consumption of gas beyond this limit will raise an exception and the state will be rolled back after consuming all the gas that was sent along with the original function. It is therefore important to test your fallback function to ensure that it does not consume more than 2,300 gas.

It is also worth noting that fallback functions are one of the top causes of security lapses in smart contracts. It is very important to test this function from a security perspective before releasing a contract on production.

Let's now try to understand the fallback function with the help of some examples.

We will use the same example as we used for explaining the call function of the address data type. However, this time, we have implemented a payable fallback function in the EtherBox contract whose entire purpose is to raise an event and an additional function that calls an invalid function. The event is also declared within the function. We will look at events in more depth in the next chapter.

When you execute each of the methods in the `UsingCall` contract, you should notice that the fallback function is not invoked for any of the functions apart from one that does not call a correct function, as shown in the following screenshot:

```solidity
pragma solidity ^0.4.17;

contract EtherBox {
    uint balance;
    event logme(string);

    function SetBalance() public {
        balance = balance + 10;
    }

    function GetBalance() public payable returns(uint) {
        return balance;
    }

    function() payable {
        logme("fallback called");
    }
}

contract UsingCall {
    function UsingCall() public payable  {
    }

    function SimpleCall() public returns (uint) {
        bool status = true;
        EtherBox eb = new EtherBox();
        address myaddr = address(eb);
        status =   myaddr.call(bytes4(sha3("SetBalance()")));
        return eb.GetBalance();
    }

    function SimpleCallwithGas() public returns (bool) {
        bool status = true;
        EtherBox eb = new EtherBox();
        address myaddr = address(eb);
        return status =   myaddr.call.gas(200000)(bytes4(sha3("GetBalance()")));
    }

    function SimpleCallwithGasAndValue() public returns (bool) {
        bool status = true;
        EtherBox eb = new EtherBox();
        address myaddr = address(eb);
        return status =   myaddr.call.gas(200000).value(1)(bytes4(sha3("GetBalance()")));
    }

    function SimpleCallwithGasAndValueWithWrongName() public returns (bool) {
        bool status = true;
        EtherBox eb = new EtherBox();
        address myaddr = address(eb);
        return myaddr.call.gas(200000).value(1)(bytes4(sha3("GetBalance1()")));
    }
}
```

Fallback functions are also invoked when using the `send` method, using the `web3` `SendTransaction` function, or the `transfer` method.

Summary

Once again, this was a heavy chapter that focused primarily on functions, including the `address` functions and the `pure`, `constant`, and `view` functions. The `address` functions can be intimidating, especially when you consider their multiple variations and their relationship with the fallback functions. If you are implementing a fallback function, remember to pay special attention to testing, especially from a security point of view. You should also pay special attention when using low-level Solidity functions such as `send`, `call`, and `transfer` as they invoke the fallback function implicitly. Always try using contract functions that use ABI as it ensures that the proper function, along with its data types, is being called.

In the next chapter, we will dive deep into the world of events, logging, and exception handling in Solidity. Stay tuned!

8
Exceptions, Events, and Logging

Writing contracts is the fundamental purpose of Solidity. However, writing a contract demands sound error and exception handling. Errors and exceptions are the norm in programming and Solidity provides ample infrastructure for managing both. Writing robust contracts with proper error and exception management is one of the top best practices. Events are another important construct in Solidity. For all topics that we've discussed so far, we've seen a caller that invokes functions in contracts; however we have not discussed any mechanism through which a contract notifies its caller and others about changes in its state and otherwise. This is where events come in. Events are a part of event-driven programs where, based on changes within a program, it proactively notifies its caller about the changes. The caller is free to use this information or ignore it. Finally, both exceptions and events, to a large extent, use the logging feature provided by EVM.

In this chapter, we will cover the following topics:

- Understanding exception handling in Solidity
- Error handling with `require`
- Error handling with `assert`
- Error handling with `revert`
- Understanding events
- Declaring an event
- Using an event
- Writing to logs

Error handling

Errors are often inadvertently introduced while writing contracts, so writing robust contracts is a good practice and should be followed. Errors are a fact of life in the programming world and writing error-free contracts is a desired skill. Errors can occur at design time or runtime. Solidity is compiled into bytecode and there are design-level checks for any syntax errors at design time while compiling. Runtime errors, however, are more difficult to catch and generally occur while executing contracts. It is important to test the contract for possible runtime errors, but it is more important to write defensive and robust contracts that take care of both design time and runtime errors.

Examples of runtime errors are out-of-gas errors, divide by zero errors, data type overflow errors, array-out-of-index errors, and so on.

Until version 4.10 of Solidity there was a single `throw` statement available for error handling. Developers had to write multiple `if...else` statements to check the values and throw in the case of an error. The `throw` statement consumes all the provided gas and reverts to the original state. This is not an ideal situation for architects and developers as unused gas should be returned back to the caller.

From version 4.10 of Solidity newer error handling constructs were introduced and `throw` was made obsolete. These were the `assert`, `require`, and `revert` statements. In this section, we will look into these error handling constructs.

It is worth noting that there are no `try..catch` statements or constructs to catch errors and exceptions.

The require statement

The word require denotes constraints. Declaring `require` statements means declaring prerequisites for running the function; in other words, it means declaring constraints that should be satisfied before executing the following lines of code.

The `require` statement takes in a single argument: a statement that evaluates to a `true` or `false` boolean value. If the evaluation of the statement is `false`, an exception is raised and execution is halted. The unused gas is returned to the caller and the state is reversed to the original. The `require` statement results in the `revert` opcode, which is responsible for reverting the state and returning unused gas.

The following code illustrates use of the `require` statement:

```solidity
pragma solidity ^0.4.19;

contract RequireContract {

    function ValidInt8(uint _data) public returns(uint8){
        require(_data >= 0);
        require(_data <= 255);

        return uint8(_data);
    }

    function ShouldbeEven(uint _data) public returns(bool){
        require(_data % 2 == 0);
        return true;
    }

}
```

Let's take a look at the following functions depicted in the preceding screenshot:

1. `ValidInt8`: This function uses a couple of `require` statements. In constructs, a statement checks for values greater than or equal to zero. If this statement is `true`, execution passes to the next statement. If this statement is `false`, an exception is thrown and execution stops. The next `require` statement checks whether the value is less than or equal to `255`. If the argument is greater than `255`, the statement evaluates to `false` and throws an exception.

2. `ShouldbeEven`: This function is of a similar nature. In this function, `require` checks whether the incoming argument is even or odd. If the argument is even, execution passes to the next statement; otherwise an exception is thrown.

The `require` statement should be used for validating all arguments and values that are incoming to the function. This means that if another function from another contract or function in the same contract is called, the incoming value should also be checked using the `require` function. The `require` function should be used to check the current state of variables before they are used. If `require` throws an exception, it should mean that the values passed to the function were not expected by the function and that the caller should modify the value before sending it to a contract.

The assert statement

The `assert` statement has a similar syntax to the `require` statement. If it accepts a statement, that should then evaluate to either a true or false value. Based on that, the execution will either move on to the next statement or throw an exception. The unused gas is not returned to the caller and instead the entire gas supply is consumed by `assert`. The state is reversed to original. The `assert` function results in invalid opcode, which is responsible for reverting the state and consuming all gas.

The function shown previously has been extended to include an addition to the existing variable. However, remember that adding two variables can result in an overflow exception. This is verified using the `assert` statement; if it returns `true`, the value is returned, otherwise the exception is thrown.

The following screenshot illustrates the use of the `assert` function:

```
pragma solidity ^0.4.19;

contract AssertContract {

    function ValidInt8(uint _data) public returns(uint8){
        require(_data >= 0);
        require(_data <= 255);

        uint8 value = 20;

        //checking datatype overflow
        assert (value + _data <= 255);

        return uint8(value + _data);
    }
}
```

While `require` should be used for values coming from the outside, `assert` should be used for validating the current state and condition of the function and contract before execution. Think of `assert` as working with runtime exceptions that you cannot predict. The `assert` statement should be used when you think that a current state has become inconsistent and that execution should not continue.

The revert statement

The revert statement is very similar to the require function. However, it does not evaluate any statement and does not depend on any state or statements. Hitting a revert statement means an exception is thrown, along with the return of unused gas, and reverts to its original state.

In the following example, an exception is thrown when the incoming value is checked using the if condition; if the if condition evaluation results in false, it executes the revert function. This results in an exception and execution stops, as shown in the following screenshot:

```
pragma solidity ^0.4.19;

contract RevertContract {

    function ValidInt8(int _data) public returns(uint8){

        if(_data < 0 || _data > 255) {
            revert();
        }

        return uint8(_data);
    }
}
```

Events and logging

We have seen the usage of events in previous chapters without going into any detail. In this section, however, we will look into events in more depth. Events are well known to event-driven programmers. Events refer to certain changes in contracts that raise events and notify each other such that they can act and execute other functions.

Events help us write asynchronous applications. Instead of continuously polling the Ethereum ledger for the existence of a transaction and then blocking with certain information, the same procedure can be implemented using events. This way, the Ethereum platform will inform the client if an event has been raised. This helps when writing modular code and also conserves resources.

Events are part of contract inheritance, where a child contract can invoke events. Event data is stored along with block data. The `logsBloom` value is the event data, as shown in the following screenshot:

```
{
  difficulty: 637123,
  extraData: "0xd78301070284676574688567f312e398777696e646f646f7773",
  gasLimit: 4712388,
  gasUsed: 44031,
  hash: "0x778b9a9a89b4609475dcc52d4c60de44254c24f8356b4886496488f57761ca0c",
  logsBloom: "0x00000000000000000000000000000000000000000000000000000000000000000000000000000000000000000000000000
00000000000000000000000000000000000000000000000000000000000008000000000000000000000000000000000000000000000000
00100000000000000000000040000000000000000000000000000000000000000000000000000000001000000000000000000040000000000
0000000000000000000000000400000000000000000000000000000000000000000000000000000000000080000",
  miner: "0xa57de277ede9c1521f51f6989ed2497a5b9c1926",
  mixHash: "0xca19a4b24b33117279d6086fe5d7d02eb2ff6cdb4332dd44289adc6d2c0e45b2",
  nonce: "0x216fd0e799898c91",
  number: 24864,
  parentHash: "0x903a7fe10d3c18e25747cc5de4425daa98baba2a0b5ccafbb768c7625461f0c3",
  receiptsRoot: "0xb428274a16608c7b00d2b36e9ddb6cff8ddaf69cc7d3e8ee52fcd2263ca679ba",
  sha3Uncles: "0x1dcc4de8dec75d7aab85b567b6ccd41ad312451b948a7413f0a142fd40d49347",
  size: 753,
  stateRoot: "0xf1196319d1d844b106a7450529aea01b7746d668ecb57060cb41eb8ddf3bb949",
  timestamp: 1516391719,
  totalDifficulty: 17314125717,
  transactions: ["0x38ca3d4b40f8e75d27ab3950234d837e96dbdd086178f139c4e675dc6531ee15"],
  transactionsRoot: "0x2442a99a90673c05a38795a711ed85f941b8116e4febee62b544fcc5f1199e43",
  uncles: []
}
```

Declaring events in Solidity is very similar to performing functions. However, events do not have any body. A simple event can be declared using the `event` keyword followed by an identifier and any parameters it wants to send along with the event as shown in the following code:

```
event LogFunctionFlow(string);
```

In the preceding line of code, `event` is the keyword used for declaring events followed by its name and a set of parameters that will be sent along with the event. Any string text can be sent with the `LogFunctionFlow` event.

Using an event is quite simple. Simply invoke an event using its name and pass on the arguments it expects. For the `LogFunctionFlow` event, the invocation would look as follows which is similar to a function call with parameters:

```
LogFunctionFlow("I am within function x");
```

The following code snippet shows an event in use. In this example, an event, `LogFunctionFlow` , is declared with a string as its sole parameter. The same event is invoked multiple times from the `ValidInt8` function, providing text information during various stages within the function:

```solidity
pragma solidity ^0.4.19;

contract EventContract {

    event LogFunctionFlow(string);

    function ValidInt8(int _data) public returns(uint8){
        LogFunctionFlow("Within function ValidInt8");

        if(_data < 0 || _data > 255) {
            revert();
        }

        LogFunctionFlow("Value is within expected range");
        LogFunctionFlow("Returning value from function");

        return uint8(_data);
    }
}
```

Executing this contract in Remix shows the result, which contains three logs with event information as shown in the following screenshot:

```
logs    [
            {
                "topic": "b5b850034705238ab6360bdc803e9e3dcaaf926c812b20193e2e99a5918d47b0",
                "event": "LogFunctionFlow",
                "args": [
                        "Within function ValidInt8"
                ]
            },
            {
                "topic": "b5b850034705238ab6360bdc803e9e3dcaaf926c812b20193e2e99a5918d47b0",
                "event": "LogFunctionFlow",
                "args": [
                        "Value is within expected range"
                ]
            },
            {
                "topic": "b5b850034705238ab6360bdc803e9e3dcaaf926c812b20193e2e99a5918d47b0",
                "event": "LogFunctionFlow",
                "args": [
                        "Returning value from function"
                ]
            }
        ]
```

Events can also be watched from custom applications and decentralized applications using web3.

 Events can be filtered using parameters names.

The following two methods allow us to watch for events:

1. **Watching individual events**: In this method, using web3, individual events from contracts can be watched and tracked. When the exact event is fired from a contract, it helps execute a function in the web3 client. An example of watching an individual event is shown in the following screenshot. Here, ageRead is the name of the event we are interested in and watching for. We read fromBlock number 25000 until the latest block. First, a reference to the ageRead event is made and a watcher is added to the reference. The watcher takes a promise function that is executed whenever the ageRead event is fired:

```
var myEvent = instance.ageRead({fromBlock: 25000, toBlock: 'latest'});
myEvent.watch(function(error, result){
    if(error) {
        console.log(error);
    }
    console.log(result.args)
});
```

2. **Watching all events**: In this method, using web3 all events from contracts can be watched and tracked. When any event is fired from a contract, it notifies and helps to execute a function in the web3 client in response. In this case, the event can be filtered using an event name. An example of watching all events is shown in the following screenshot. Here, we are interested in and watching for any event from a contract. We read fromBlock number 25000 until the latest block. First, a reference to allEvents is made and a watcher is added to the reference. The watcher then takes a promise function that is executed whenever any event is fired:

```
var myEvent = instance.allEvents({fromBlock: 24000, toBlock: 'latest'});
myEvent.watch(function(error, result){
    if(error) {
        console.log(error);
    }
    console.log(result)
});
```

The value in the `result` object from the event is shown in the following screenshot:

```
{ address: '0x600c320dd768fb55f03748d4d4028db2cafc06a9',
  blockNumber: 24864,
  transactionHash: '0x38ca3d4b40f8e75d27ab3950234d837e96dbdd086178f139c4e675dc6531ee15',
  transactionIndex: 0,
  blockHash: '0x778b9a9a89b4609475dcc52d4c60de44254c24f8356b4886496488f57761ca0c',
  logIndex: 0,
  removed: false,
  event: 'ageRead',
  args: { '': '33' } }
```

Summary

In this chapter, we covered exception handling and events. These are important topics in Solidity, especially when writing any serious decentralized applications on the Ethereum platform. Exception handling in Solidity is implemented using three functions: `assert`, `require`, and `revert`. Although they sound similar, they have different purposes, which were explained in this chapter with the help of examples. Events help us write scalable applications. Instead of continuously polling the platform for data and wasting resources, it's better to write events and then wait for them to execute functions asynchronously. This was also covered in this chapter.

In the next chapter, we will focus on using Truffle, one of the most popular development platforms for developing an application on the Ethereum platform. Stay tuned!

Truffle Basics and Unit Testing 9

Programming languages need a rich ecosystem of tools that eases development. Like any application, even blockchain based decentralized applications should have a minimal **Application Lifecycle Management** (**ALM**) process. It is important for any application to have a process of build, test, and deploy continuously. Solidity is a programming language and needs support from other tools to ensure that developers can develop, build, test, and deploy contracts with ease rather than going through the painful process of deploying and testing them. This improves their productivity and eventually helps bring the application to market faster, better, and cheaper. It is also possible to introduce DevOps for smart contracts with the help of such tools. Truffle is one such development, testing, and deployment utility that can make these activities a breeze.

This chapter covers the following topics:

- Application development life cycle management
- Understanding and installing Truffle
- Contract development with Truffle
- Testing contracts with Truffle

Application development life cycle management

As mentioned before, every serious application has some development process built around it. Typically, it involves designing, building, testing, and deploying. The contract ALM is no different from any other software or programming development life cycle. The first step in contract development is to get and finalize requirements about the problem under consideration. Requirements form the starting activity for any decentralized application. Requirements contain descriptions of problems, use cases, and detailed testing strategy.

Architects take functional and technical requirements as their inputs and create application architecture and design. They also document them using notations easily understandable by others. The project development team takes these architecture and design documents and breaks them down into features and sprints. The development team starts working on building contracts and other artifacts based on this documentation. The contracts are frequently deployed to a test environment for testing and to ensure that they are in a working condition, both technically and functionally. The contracts are unit tested to check their functionality in isolation. If there are unit test failures, the entire build and test process should be repeated. At the end, all artifacts are deployed to the production environment.

As you can see, ALM is an involved process and can consume substantial time and productivity on the part of developers. There is a need for tools and automation to help ease this process, and this is where Truffle as a utility shines.

Truffle

Truffle is an accelerator that helps increase the speed of development, deployment and testing, and increases developer productivity. It is built specifically for Ethereum-based contract and application development. The latest Truffle version is 4. It is a node runtime-based framework that can help implement DevOps, continuous integration, continuous delivery, and continuous deployment with ease.

Installing Truffle is quite simple— a prerequisite for installing Truffle is Node.js, as it is deployed as a node package.

Truffle can be installed by executing the following npm command from the command line:

```
$ npm install -g truffle
```

Here npm refers to node package manager and the -g switch signifies installation at global scope. The following screenshot shows the installation of Truffle on Windows Server 2016. The command is the same for Linux distribution as well:

Running `truffle --version` shows the current version and all commands available with Truffle as shown in the following screenshot:

```
Administrator: Command Prompt                                              —   □   ×
C:\Users\citynextadmin>truffle --version
Truffle v4.0.6 - a development framework for Ethereum

Usage: truffle <command> [options]

Commands:
  init       Initialize new and empty Ethereum project
  compile    Compile contract source files
  migrate    Run migrations to deploy contracts
  deploy     (alias for migrate)
  build      Execute build pipeline (if configuration present)
  test       Run JavaScript and Solidity tests
  debug      Interactively debug any transaction on the blockchain (experimental)
  opcode     Print the compiled opcodes for a given contract
  console    Run a console with contract abstractions and commands available
  develop    Open a console with a local development blockchain
  create     Helper to create new contracts, migrations and tests
  install    Install a package from the Ethereum Package Registry
  publish    Publish a package to the Ethereum Package Registry
  networks   Show addresses for deployed contracts on each network
  watch      Watch filesystem for changes and rebuild the project automatically
  serve      Serve the build directory on localhost and watch for changes
  exec       Execute a JS module within this Truffle environment
  unbox      Download a Truffle Box, a pre-built Truffle project
  version    Show version number and exit
```

Development with Truffle

Using Truffle is quite simple. Truffle provides lots of scaffolding code and configuration by default. Developers need only to reconfigure some of the out-of-the-box configuration options and focus on writing their contracts. Let's take a look at the following steps:

1. The first step is to create a `project` folder that will hold all projects- and Truffle-generated artifacts.

2. Navigate to that folder and enter the `init` command. The `init` command refers to the initiation and initialization of Truffle within the folder. It will generate appropriate folders, code files, configuration, and linkage within the folder as shown in the following screenshot:

```
C:\>mkdir TruffleProject

C:\>cd TruffleProject

C:\TruffleProject>truffle init
Downloading...
Unpacking...
Setting up...
Unbox successful. Sweet!

Commands:

  Compile:        truffle compile
  Migrate:        truffle migrate
  Test contracts: truffle test
```

The preceding code results in a generated folder structure as shown in the following screenshot:

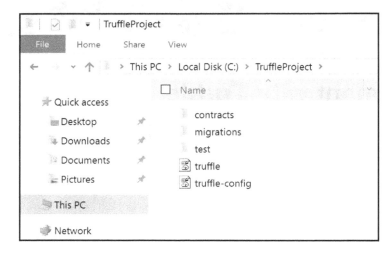

Let's take a look at the following folders shown in the preceding screenshot:

- The `contracts` folder contains a single file named `migrations.sol`. It contains a contract responsible for deploying custom contracts to an Ethereum network. Any custom contracts should be placed within this folder.
- The `migrations` folder contains multiple JavaScript files for executing the contract deployment process. These JavaScript files should be modified to ensure that all custom contracts are visible to Truffle and Truffle can chain and link them in appropriate order for deployment. It contains multiple JavaScript files prefixed with a number. These scripts are executed in a consecutive order starting from 1.
- The `test` folder is empty but any custom test scripts should be placed within this folder.
- There are two JSON configuration files—`truffle` and `truffle-config`. The main configuration file of interest for a project is `truffle.js` and this should be customized for the project. It should export a JSON object such that Truffle runtime can use it to configure the environment.

An important configuration information that should be provided here is the network information to which Truffle should connect and deploy contracts.

3. The following code snippet can be used to configure the network configuration. There should be an existing Geth instance running with an RPC endpoint and port enabled; ganache-cli can also be used instead of geth for deploying contracts using the JSON-RPC protocol. A network configuration element should be defined to connect to an existing Ethereum network. The network is configured with a name and, similarly, multiple networks can be configured for different environments:

```
module.exports = {
    networks: {
      development: {
          host: "127.0.0.1",
          port: 8545,
          network_id: "*" // Match any network id
      }
    }
};
```

4. Create a new contract and store it within the `contracts` folder with `first.sol` as filename and content, as shown in the following screenshot:

```
pragma solidity ^0.4.17;
contract First {
        int public mydata;
        function GetDouble(int _data) public returns (int
_output) {
                mydata = _data * 2;
                return _data * 2;
        }
    }
```

5. Write another contract as shown in the following screenshot and save it in the same folder as earlier with `second.sol` as the filename:

```
pragma solidity ^0.4.17;
import "./first.sol";
        contract Second {
                address firstAddress;
                int public _data;
                function Second(address _first) public {
                    firstAddress = _first;
                }
            function SetData() public {
                First h = First(firstAddress);
                _data = h.GetDouble(21);
            }
        }
```

Eventually, the `contract` folder looks as shown in the following screenshot:

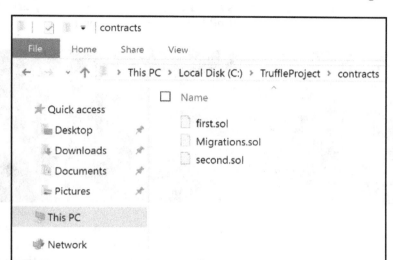

6. Modify the `migrations` folder to add another script file to it. It should be noted that each filename must be incremented by one for setting the order of deployment of contracts. In our case, the name of the file is `2_Custom.js`. The content of this file is shown next. The first two lines of this file refer to two contracts written earlier. This file exports a function that is invoked by Truffle while deploying. The function first deploys the first contract and, after successfully deploying the first contract, deploys the second contract as shown in the following screenshot:

```
var hw = artifacts.require("First");

var hw1 = artifacts.require("Second");

module.exports = function(deployer) {
   deployer.deploy(hw).then
     (function() {
         return deployer.deploy(hw1,hw.address);
     })};
```

7. Execute the `compile` command using `truffle.cmd` as shown in the following screenshot. It might give errors and a warning. If there are any errors or warnings, they should be rectified before moving ahead:

```
C:\TruffleProject>truffle.cmd compile
Compiling .\contracts\First.sol...
Compiling .\contracts\Migrations.sol...
Compiling .\contracts\first.sol...
Compiling .\contracts\second.sol...

Compilation warnings encountered:

/C/TruffleProject/contracts/second.sol:9:5: Warning: No visibility specified. Defaulting to "public".
    function Second(address _first) {
    ^
Spanning multiple lines.

Writing artifacts to .\build\contracts
```

It is to be noted that on Windows, when executing the `truffle` command on Windows, if it gives an error related to an undefined module, you should execute `truffle.cmd`, instead of just `truffle`, with the command.

8. Now it's time to deploy the compiled contracts. Truffle provides the `migrate` command and it should be used as shown in the following screenshot. It is to be noted, that before running the `migrate` command, an instance of Geth or ganache-cli should be running. In case of using Geth mining, the mining process should also be running. If using `testrpc`, miners are not required:

```
C:\TruffleProject>truffle.cmd migrate
Using network 'development'.

Running migration: 1_initial_migration.js
  Deploying Migrations...
  ... 0x262e57282d269620a6642f6f5806ec72f0917d48979747d1cad9cb2106009a68
  Migrations: 0x65989fd1cdb5813460258a80c406ec25e00871a3
Saving successful migration to network...
  ... 0x7282c4bdde56076beaecd71785198ec2b93fd788a126ad40c06c37105d39402d
Saving artifacts...
Running migration: 2_Custom.js
  Deploying First...
  ... 0x3f507f2ecdc8842ca6f149d532401cfa7e325425960041dddb942e64381d7960
  First: 0xcf52edb0f5e9fd1509e5446b7c09889e0f3beb15
  Deploying Second...
  ... 0xc4bde155b2379d0ec8760e2da238dda96de6448291ae4410d98fef8e951df9a2
  Second: 0x7f3231d099966966230f1a0437d89f8824dc97db
Saving successful migration to network...
  ... 0x711f4234786b06542a48d374e0da98e6e348afd4d68d6247058c98595b51dd3b
Saving artifacts...
```

The preceding screenshot shows that both the migration scripts were executed based on their number ordering. Now, the contracts are deployed and available for consumption. An instance of contract can be created using its ABI definition and address. The contract address along, with the transaction hash, are available.

There are many more activities and commands available with Truffle; however to keep this chapter concise, we will move towards understanding unit testing of contracts using Truffle runtime.

Testing with Truffle

Unit testing refers to a type of testing specific to a software unit and component in isolation. Unit tests help ensure that code in a contract is written according to functional and technical requirements. When each of the smallest components is tested under different scenarios and passes successfully, other important tests such as integration tests can be performed to test multiple components.

As mentioned before, Truffle generates a `test` folder and all test files should be placed in this folder. Tests can be written in JavaScript as well as Solidity. Since this is a book on Solidity, tests are focused on writing using Solidity.

Tests in Solidity are written by authoring contracts and saved as a Solidity file. The name of the contract should start with the `Test` prefix and each function within the contract should be prefixed with `test`. Please note the case sensitivity of the `Test` and the `test` prefix for both contracts as well as function names.

The following screenshot shows the code for writing tests within the contract:

```solidity
pragma solidity ^0.4.19;

import "truffle/Assert.sol";
import "truffle/DeployedAddresses.sol";
import "../contracts/first.sol";

contract TestFirst {
  function testGetDoublePositiveUsingDeployedContract() {
    First meta = First(DeployedAddresses.First());

    Assert.equal(meta.GetDouble(10), 20, "Positive input gives double value");
  }

}
```

There are a few things to note in the `TestFirst` contract. Important Truffle-provided libraries such as `Assert.sol` and `DeployedAddresses.sol` are imported so that functions in them can be used.

There can be multiple functions within one contract but for demonstration purposes a single unit test is written. In practice there will be multiple tests within the same contract.

The first line in the function creates a reference to the deployed `First` contract and invokes the `GetDouble` function. The `return` value from this function is compared to the second parameter of the `Assert.equal` function and, if both are the same, then the test succeeds; otherwise it fails.

The `Assert.equal` function helps compare an actual return value with the expected return value.

It is important to understand that, whenever a function within a contract is invoked, it is a transaction that will eventually be written in a block and ledger. In effect, testing a function within a contract also means that you are testing transactions related to your smart contract.

Tests are executed using the `test` command as shown in the following screenshot:

```
C:\TruffleProject>truffle.cmd test
Using network 'development'.

Compiling .\contracts\first.sol...
Compiling .\test\TestFirst.sol...
Compiling truffle/Assert.sol...
Compiling truffle/DeployedAddresses.sol...

Compilation warnings encountered:

/C/TruffleProject/test/TestFirst.sol:10:3: Warning: No visibility specified. Defaulting to "public".
  function testGetDoublePositiveUsingDeployedContract() {
  ^
Spanning multiple lines.


  TestFirst
    √ testGetDoublePositiveUsingDeployedContract (110ms)


  1 passing (859ms)
```

Summary

This chapter introduced Truffle as a utility for easing the processes of authoring, testing, and deploying Solidity contracts. Instead of typing and executing each step, Truffle provides easy commands for compiling, deploying, and testing contracts.

The following chapter will be the last chapter of this book and will focus on troubleshooting activities and tools related to Solidity. Debugging is an important aspect of troubleshooting and is an important skill for any contract developer and development. Remix debugging facilities will be discussed along with other mechanisms for debugging contracts.

10
Debugging Contracts

This is the last chapter of the book. By now, we have looked at Solidity and Ethereum from a conceptual standpoint, developed and authored Solidity contracts, and tested them. The only thing that was not discussed was troubleshooting contracts. Troubleshooting is an important skill and exercise when dealing with any programming language. It helps in finding issues and solving them efficiently. Troubleshooting is both an art and a science. Developers should learn the art of troubleshooting through experience as well as by exploring details behind the scenes using debugging. This chapter will focus on debugging coding issues related to Solidity contracts.

This chapter covers the following topics:

- Debugging contracts
- Debugging contracts using Remix and Solidity events

Debugging

Debugging is an important exercise when authoring Solidity smart contracts. Debugging refers to finding issues, bugs, and removing them by changing code. It is very difficult to debug a smart contract if there is in adequate support from tools and utilities. Generally, debugging involves executing each line of code step by step, finding the current state of temporary, local, and global variables and walking through each instruction while executing contracts.

There are the following ways to debug Solidity contracts:

- Using the Remix editor
- Events
- Block explorer

The Remix editor

We used the Remix editor to write Solidity contracts in the previous chapters. However, we have not used the debugging utility available in Remix. The Remix debugger helps us observe the runtime behavior of contract execution and identify issues. The debugger works in Solidity and the resultant contract bytecode. With the debugger, the execution can be paused to examine contract code, state variables, local variables, and stack variables, and view the EVM instructions generated from contract code.

The following screenshot of contract code will be used to demonstrate debugging using the Remix editor:

```solidity
pragma solidity ^0.4.0;

contract DebuggerSampleContract {

    int counter = 10;

    function LoopCounter(int _input) public view returns (int)  {
        int returnValue;

        for (; _input < counter; _input ++)
        {
            returnValue  += _input;
        }
        return returnValue;
    }
}
```

The contract has a single state variable and function. The function loops over the provided input till it reaches the value of `counter` and returns a cumulative sum to the caller.

Deploying and executing the `LoopCounter` function will provide an opportunity to debug this function by clicking on the **Debug** button as shown in the following screenshot:

```
creation of DebuggerSampleContract pending...

[vm] from:0xca3...a733c, to:DebuggerSampleContract.(constructor), value:0 we      [ Details ]  [ Debug ]
i, data:0x606...d0029, 0 logs, hash:0x719...ab533
```

This will bring the focus to the **Debugger** tab in Remix and here runtime information about local, state, memory, callstack, stack, instructions, and call data can be verified for the execution of each code step.

The following next two screenshots show varied internal information about contract runtime execution:

Take a look at the second screenshot, as follows:

The following instructions from the preceding screenshot show the bytecode for function execution:

- **Solidity Locals**: This instruction shows the incoming parameter, data type, and its value.
- **Solidity State**: This instruction shows the state variables, their data type, and current value.
- **Step detail**: This is important for debugging gas usage, consumption, and remaining gas.
- **Call Stack**: This instruction shows the interim variables needed by function code.
- **Memory**: This instruction shows the local variables used within the function.
- **Call Data**: This function shows the actual payload the client sends to the contract. The first four bytes refer to the function identifier and the rest contain 32 bytes for each incoming parameter.

An important aspect of debugging is to stop the execution at each line of code of special interest. Breakpoints help do this. Clicking on any line beside the line number helps in setting up a breakpoint. Clicking again removes the breakpoint. During the execution of a function, when it hits this line; the execution is halted, and the values and execution can be verified from the **Debugger** tab. The following screenshot shows the breakpoint:

```solidity
 3    pragma solidity ^0.4.0;
 4
 5 ▾  contract DebuggerSampleContract {
 6
 7        int counter = 10;
 8
 9 ▾      function LoopCounter(int _input) public view returns (int)  {
10            int returnValue;
11
12            for (; _input < counter; _input ++)
13 ▾          {
14                returnValue  += _input;
15            }
16            return returnValue;
17        }
18    }
```

Using Remix, it is also possible to perform Step over back, Step back, Step into, Step over forward, Jump to the previous breakpoint, Jump out, and Jump to the next breakpoint. It also provides the facility to view information using a block number or transaction hash about a particular block or transaction. It is possible to provide a transaction number in a block instead of a transaction hash, as shown in the following screenshot:

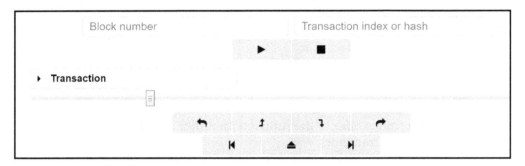

Using events

We saw how to use events in Chapter 8, *Exceptions, Events, and Logging*. Events can be trapped and can help provide relevant information about the current execution. Contracts should declare events and functions should invoke these events at appropriate locations with information that provides enough context to whoever is reading these events.

Using a Block Explorer

A Block Explorer is an Ethereum browser. It provides reports and information about current blocks and transactions in its network. It's a great place to learn more about existing and past data. It is available at https://etherscan.io/, as shown in the following screenshot:

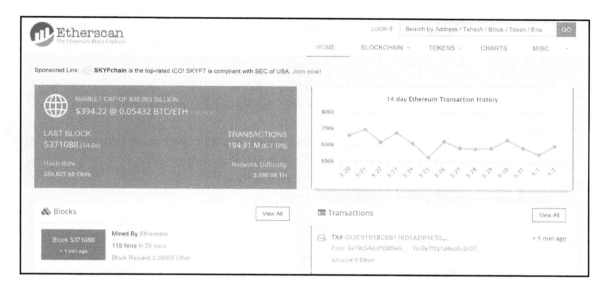

It shows transactions involving both accounts and contracts. Clicking on a transaction shows details about it, as shown in the following screenshot:

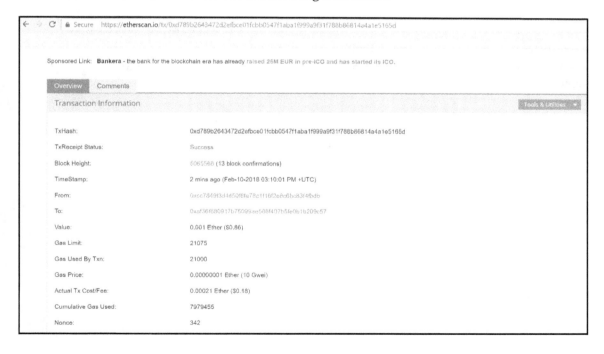

By now, you understand the details about transactions stored within the Ethereum ledger. From the preceding screenshot, let's take a look at the following few details of the transaction:

- **TxHash:** This detail refers to transaction hashes
- **TxReceipt Status**: This detail represents the status of a transaction, whether successful or pending
- **Block Height**: This detail shows which block number the transaction is stored in
- **TimeStamp**: This detail shows the timestamp for the transaction
- **From**: This detail shows who sent the transaction
- **To**: This detail shows the recipient of the transaction
- **Value**: This details shows the amount of Ether transferred
- **Gas Limit**: This detail represents the gas limit specified by the user
- **Gas Used By Txn**: This detail shows the amount of gas used by the transaction
- **Gas Price**: This detail shows an amount of gas price determined by the sender
- **nonce**: This is to determine the count of transactions sent by the sender
- **Actual Tx Cost/Fees**: This detail shows total cost of a transaction, that is, gas used * gas price

Clicking on a block shows information about the block and a list of transactions that are part of that block. It shows all the details from a block header, such as block hash, parent hash, miner account, difficulty level, nonce, and more, as shown in the following screenshot:

The block header has some interesting properties, and some of them are mentioned here. The **Height** detail provides the block number in the ledger, the number of transactions within the block (110 in this case), and the number of internal transactions (these are referred to as message calls between contracts), the hash of current block header (**Hash**), the hash of the parent block (**Parent Hash**), the hash of the root for uncles, the coinbase or etherbase account that mined the block (**Mined By**), the difficulty level for the current block, the cumulative difficulty for all blocks till the current block, the size of the block, the total gas used by all transactions within the block, the maximum limit of gas for the block, the evidence that proof of work has been carried out (**Nonce**), and the reward for mining the block.

Summary

This brings us to the end of this chapter and this book. Solidity is a new programming language that is evolving continuously. Solidity contracts can be debugged using the Remix editor. Remix provides a convenient way to author and debug contracts by verifying variables and code execution at every step. It helps us move forward and back in code execution. It provides breakpoints to break the execution of code. There are other ways to debug contracts as well. These include using Block Explorers and Solidity events. Although events and Block Explorers provide limited capabilities for debugging, they are very helpful and facilitate production.

I hope you enjoyed reading this book and sincerely believe that you are becoming a rock star Solidity developer by now. Stay tuned and keep learning!

Other Books You May Enjoy

If you enjoyed this book, you may be interested in these other books by Packt:

Mastering Blockchain - Second Edition
Imran Bashir

ISBN: 978-1-78883-904-4

- Master the theoretical and technical foundations of the blockchain technology
- Understand the concept of decentralization, its impact, and its relationship with blockchain technology
- Master how cryptography is used to secure data - with practical examples
- Grasp the inner workings of blockchain and the mechanisms behind bitcoin and alternative cryptocurrencies
- Understand the theoretical foundations of smart contracts
- Learn how Ethereum blockchain works and how to develop decentralized applications using Solidity and relevant development frameworks
- Identify and examine applications of the blockchain technology - beyond currencies
- Investigate alternative blockchain solutions including Hyperledger, Corda, and many more
- Explore research topics and the future scope of blockchain technology

Building Blockchain Projects

Narayan Prusty

ISBN: 978-1-78712-214-7

- Walk through the basics of the Blockchain technology
- Implement Blockchain's technology and its features, and see what can be achieved using them
- Build DApps using Solidity and Web3.js
- Understand the geth command and cryptography
- Create Ethereum wallets
- Explore consortium blockchain

Leave a review - let other readers know what you think

Please share your thoughts on this book with others by leaving a review on the site that you bought it from. If you purchased the book from Amazon, please leave us an honest review on this book's Amazon page. This is vital so that other potential readers can see and use your unbiased opinion to make purchasing decisions, we can understand what our customers think about our products, and our authors can see your feedback on the title that they have worked with Packt to create. It will only take a few minutes of your time, but is valuable to other potential customers, our authors, and Packt. Thank you!

Index

www.ingramcontent.com/pod-product-compliance
Lightning Source LLC
Chambersburg PA
CBHW080524060326
40690CB00022B/5022

* 9 7 8 1 7 8 8 8 3 1 3 8 3 *